George Washington Brown

The Truth At Last

History Corrected

George Washington Brown

The Truth At Last
History Corrected

ISBN/EAN: 9783337113353

Printed in Europe, USA, Canada, Australia, Japan

Cover: Foto ©ninafisch / pixelio.de

More available books at **www.hansebooks.com**

CAPT. JOHN BROWN.

The Truth at Last. History Corrected.

REMINISCENCES

OF

OLD JOHN BROWN.

THRILLING INCIDENTS

OF

BORDER LIFE IN KANSAS;

WITH AN APPENDIX,

CONTAINING STATEMENTS, AND FULL DETAILS OF THE POTTAWOTOMIE MASSACRE, BY GOV. CRAWFORD, COL. BLOOD, JAS. TOWNSLEY, COL. WALKER, AND OTHERS, TO WHICH IS ADDED

A REVIEW: BY HON. ELI THAYER, OF MASSACHUSETTS.

BY G. W. BROWN, M. D.

Where thou findest a lie that is oppressing thee extinguish it. Lies exist only to be extinguished. They wait and cry earnestly for extinction. Think well, meanwhile, in what spirit thou wilt do it; not with hatred; not with headlong, selfish violence; but in clearness of heart, with holy zeal, gently, almost with pity.—CARLYLE.

Let Truth and Falsehood grapple. Who ever knew Truth put to the worse in a free and open encounter?—MILTON.

ROCKFORD, ILLINOIS:
STEREOTYPED AND PRINTED BY ABRAHAM E. SMITH.
1880.

Entered according to Act of Congress, in the year 1879.

By G. W. BROWN, M. D.,

In the Office of the Librarian of Congress, at Washington, D. C.

[All Rights Reserved.]

DEDICATION.

To the HISTORICAL SOCIETY OF KANSAS, these humble pages are respectfully dedicated. They have been written at the request of a distinguished citizen of your State, to correct any errors that have crept into your early history, from the carelessness of past writers, or from their desire to eulogize esteemed friends. I hope that neither Malice nor Misrepresentation has guided my pen.

It has been truly said that the early history of all nations is founded in myth, as is that of the world in fable. The American States, though their origin is so recent, are not exceptions; and even Kansas, with an organized existence but little exceeding twenty-five years, is subject to a like condition. Already she begins to substitute fiction and legend for facts. Already she is weaving chaplets to adorn the brows of gods whom she has apotheosized. As one of your oldest journalists, identified with all your early history, and an eye witness of many of the incidents narrated, it seems highly proper that I should aid you in your very laudable endeavor to TRANSMIT ONLY TRUTH TO POSTERITY.

Rockford, Ill., January 15, 1880. THE AUTHOR.

INTRODUCTION

In September, 1879, the author of these pages, by special invitation, attended the celebration of the Old Settlers of Kansas, held at Bismarck Grove, near Lawrence, in commemoration of the 25th anniversary of the founding of that State. He heard repeatedly, during the two days the convention was in session, the principal character in these pages, lauded as the person of all others to whom Kansas is indebted for her rescue from slavery. He learned that a monument had been erected to his memory, at Osawotomie, and that it was proposed to send a statue of him to Washington, to adorn the National Capitol, and perpetuate his renown. He saw all around him the *real* heroes in the strife; those who a year earlier than old John Brown, had settled in Kansas; who had taken their families with them; who had sacrificed everything but honor for the triumph of a principle; who had been genuine models of the brave and true; while in imagination he turned his eye to the cemetery, where the dead martyrs repose, and he inquired of himself:—

"Must this state of things always continue? Shall they who endured all but death, and who struggled successfully to the end, ever faithful to their convictions, be pushed permanently aside to make room for those who were really destitute of merit? Shall Dow, and Barber, and Hoyt, and Shombre, and Phillips, and the other immortal dead, rest in unknown graves, while the towering shaft, the sculptured marble, and the brightest page of history emblazon the name of him who retarded our efforts, threw obstacles in the way of our success, discouraged honest endeavor, and who blackened our otherwise bloodless escutcheon with crime and death? Shall tongue remain silent, and pen at rest, while the real actors—the genuinely brave—shall die, and their memories pass into oblivion? No! Twenty years have passed since old John Brown paid the penalty of his folly and wrong-doing with his life! The time has come, if it ever will come, when the truth of history must be vindicated; when the principal facts in his Kansas adventures ought to be given to the world; when they who have been crowded aside and treated as non-entities should take the front, and wear the garlands so long adorning dishonored brows. Though other duties are pressing, and my pen has been idle for years, yet *I will write for preservation*, and leave to those who shall succeed me, what I know and believe in regard to old John Brown!"

Permeated with these feelings I returned to my home, delighted with what I had seen of the material prosperity of Kansas; grateful for the cordial welcome I had received at the hands of my old associates; and gladdened at the brilliant future awaiting this infant and central State; but mortified as I contemplated the wrongs perpetrated upon my compeers, by awarding merit where it did not belong, and leaving those entitled to the true meed of Fame to languish in obscurity, soon to pass into forgetfulness.

A few days after reaching home I received a copy of the Lawrence Journal, when my eye fell upon a marked article, and read at the head of it, "An Open Letter to Geo. W. Brown, from Gov. Robinson." "What have I done," thought I, "that I should be called to account by Gov. Robinson?" This was the first impulse. I read, and was startled with his proposition! "Wonder," thought I, "if he had the same feelings with myself at

Bismarck Grove? Wonder if, as he looked over that vast assembly, as its presiding officer, and back over the darkened history of Kansas, and thought of the mouldering dead who laid down their lives that Freedom might live, and heard eulogy on eulogy, the sweet voice of song, and the loud trump of Fame, all enlisted in favor of a single person whose name is hardly worthy of preservation,—wonder if he felt as I in regard to that character?"

I took my pen and hurriedly answered. The two letters,—that of Gov. Robinson, and my own in reply,—are on the following pages, and the product of his request, so far as relates to John Brown, constitutes the substance of this humble volume.

I hope some day to re-write it, and correct such errors as my attention has been or may be called to, by personal friends and gentlemanly critics, or which the malice of bitter enemies may point out.

CORRESPONDENCE.

LAWRENCE, KANSAS, September 22, 1879.

DR. GEO. W. BROWN—DEAR SIR:—Your presence at the Old Settlers' Gathering, on the 15th and 16th instant, as well as your intimate connection with every movement in Kansas, in 1855, '56 and '57, has created a desire on the part of the friends of truth and history, to hear from you relative to those critical times. The Historical Society is collecting data on all matters of general interest, from the actors in the drama, but so far has nothing from you. As you were never in office, and never desired any, so far as I ever knew, and were never under obligations to active participants in the struggle, your testimony ought to be impartial. One subject seems just now to be uppermost in the minds of writers of history, and that is, where to place Gen. Lane and John Brown. One writer says: "Lane's actions and efforts in 1856 deserve the highest praise. * He was the only man the people could tie to," etc.

Another writer says: "If I were to name two men of different tastes and ambitions, to whom Kansas owes most for her deliverance from the clutches of the slave power, I would mention James H. Lane and John Brown."

And another writer says: "His services were greatly over-estimated. He also did a great deal of bad. He was the originator of the corruption in politics that Kansas is credited with. His forte was bulldozing and deceit. He killed himself because he undertook to sell Kansas out, but found he could not deliver the goods."

Still another calls him, "the greatest liar of his time," and says he should be held up as a warning to young men.

It is plain that neither their beneficiaries and partisan worshippers, nor their enemies, can be fully relied upon to do full justice to these men. A statement, to be valuable as history, should be unbiased, with nothing extenuated and nothing set down in malice.— Can you give such a statement, show what policy these men advocated, tell whether the people in critical times followed their counsels, and if it was by pursuing their lead and advice, Kansas was saved from slavery, or the reverse? This will settle the question of the value of their services better than any amount of detraction by enemies, or fulsome laudation by friends. It is not eulogy nor censure that is desired, but FACTS for the historian. Very Truly, C. ROBINSON.

REPLY.

ROCKFORD, ILLINOIS, October 10, 1879.

GOV. CHAS. ROBINSON:—Yours of the 22d ult., which I first saw in the Lawrence Journal, is at hand. You ask me to furnish facts to enable the historian to know where to place Gen. Lane and John Brown in the history of Kansas. You predicate this desire on my "intimate connection with every movement in Kansas associated with her early history, with freedom from personal or party bias, and from lack of obligation to any of the active participants in the strife."

I went to Kansas in the autumn of 1854, taking a party of nearly three hundred with me from Pennsylvania. I also took with me a large printing establishment, and *printed on Kansas soil, several days in advance of any other, the first Free State newspaper published in that Territory.*

My wife, father, mother, sister, brother, and nearest friends accompanied me. Our object was neither honor nor emoluments; but thoroughly imbued with anti-slavery sentiments, we went there to make Kansas a Free State. That end attained, my mission was ended. At the close of the war, in 1865, I bade adieu to all my early associates in Kansas, those with whom I spent eleven of the best years of my life, and located in this beautiful city, in Northern Illinois, where, probably, I shall spend the residue of my years, I trust in quiet, at peace with all the world.

About a year ago I received a letter from Hon. John Speer, stating that he was about to write a biographical history of Kansas; that my name, with others, had been selected for a place in its pages; closing by requesting a sketch of leading incidents in my life, for publication. I wrote him, substantially, in reply : "That I had no ambition to perpetuate myself in history ; that I had done the best I knew to advance the material interests of humanity ; that I had always determined the world should be better for my having lived in it ; that the stream of Time was rapidly flowing onward ; that in a very few years all would reach the great gulf of Oblivion, where we should disappear together; and that I had no motive in trying to float on its darkened bosom, conscious that in the end, my fate would be that of every other lover of his race."

While this is still my feeling, as regards myself, I recognize this fact, that "Truth is a debt which every man owes his neighbor." I also remember an axiom, by the "Author-Hero of the Revolution," that "Facts are but links in the great chain of truth." If there are missing links in the chain of Kansas history, which I have the ability to supply, connected as I was with its early settlement, in the capacity of a journalist, "All of which I saw and a part of which I was," it is my duty to do so; hence I accept of your very kind invitation, and will commence a series of articles relating to Capt. John Brown in Kansas immediately. That pertaining to Gen. Lane I will defer for a time.

I shall endeavor to state nothing but facts, as seen from my own stand-point ; will answer any pertinent questions honestly submitted with the view of arriving at truth, and will leave others to make their own deductions as to the place the names you mention deserve on the scroll of Fame. Your own intimate connection with almost every event in the early history of Kansas, will enable you to either corroborate or correct my statements, while impartial criticism, and such new light as shall be thrown upon the subjects of my sketches during their publication, will dispel much error, now honestly entertained in regard to these historic characters. Very Truly, G. W. BROWN.

PREFATORY.

For the better understanding of what shall be said in regard to the subjects of these inquiries, it may be well to inform the reader at the outset, that there were two classes of early settlers who went out to Kansas from the Northern States. Indeed, it seems just to say there were three classes.

The first of these, and by far the most numerous, were those who met the issue squarely which was presented them in the Kansas-Nebraska act. They had no other idea than to settle the question by the ballot. In short, they accepted the doctrine of "popular sovereignty," as enunciated in the organic law, and as the Missouri Compromise, prohibiting slavery North of 36 degrees, was repealed, and the question was to be settled at the polls, their ambition was to get as many pioneers as possible from the free North, whose education, prejudices, instincts, and interests were all for freedom. This idea was clearly set forth in the leading editorial in the first number of the *Herald of Freedom*, edited and published by the writer, and was the guiding principle of that paper throughout the whole period of its publication. Papers like the *Liberator*, by Wm. Lloyd Garrison; the *Anti-Slavery Standard*, under the direction of Oliver Johnson; and the *Anti-Slavery Bugle*, published at Salem, Ohio, took issue with these positions, and complained that those who followed such leaders and teachings, were fighting the battles of freedom on a low plane; that they had no right to expect success; that defeat was inevitable; that it was deserved, and that no genuine anti-slavery man could co-operate with them. Every movement in the direction of a pacific settlement of our difficulties was scouted, and stigmatized as "an attempt to sell out the Free State party," and with having "gone over to the enemy."

The second class of settlers consisted of a comparatively small number. They made up for this in activity; were mostly young men, without families or homes of their own. They were literally "carpetbaggers." Their desire was to embroil the country in war. They claimed to be genuine haters of slavery, but saw no means for its extinction save through revolution. Every opportunity was sought to influence the public mind, and incite a contest. Letters were written and books published in their interest. It required caution, coolness and great activity to foil these workers of mischief in their many bloody schemes. Actual settlers and property holders were constant sufferers because of the excesses of these men. When danger assailed the Territory, the less brave of them had business in the States; when all was pacific they would return, renew their violence, and again away.

And then the third class: They had no *principle* in the matter. They were governed wholly by selfish interests; and always acted with that wing of the party from which at the time they supposed they had most to hope. We never knew where to find them, or what to expect at their hands. To-day, perhaps, pro-slavery; to-morrow very conservative free white State Democrats, and next day rabid abolitionists; and thus varying through all phases of the question, as they supposed public sentiment had changed.

I am glad to say there were but a very limited few who occupied these latter positions. They, however, seriously embarrassed proper action at times, and their influence on more than one occasion seriously threatened the final favorable result.

EXPLANATORY.

I was called upon the next day after my Reply to Gov. Robinson, was published in the GAZETTE, by a gentleman of Rockford, who requested me to "Remember that John Brown and Jas. H. Lane are dead, and that I should be humane in the treatment of these historic characters."

My recollection coincided with my clerical friend, in regard to the death of these personages, so I replied:

"I am writing *facts* for history, and as a faithful historian I shall endeavor not to withhold anything because they are dead, that is necessary to a truthful knowledge of their real characters; and certainly shall not give anything from malice, for I held none towards either of them while living."

More than twenty years have passed since any of these events I shall narrate have occurred. I have not been identified for more than fourteen years with Kansas, her politics, individuals, or history. For nearly eleven years previous I was familiarly intimate with nearly every transaction relating to her early settlement. The Historical Society of Kansas is gathering up important events connected with those times, for preservation in her archives, before all the actors in them shall pass away. Gov. Robinson is the honored Chairman of that Society, and, as such, asks me to tell the *truth* in regard to the connection of John Brown and Gen. Lane with that history.

Is it less my duty, as a historian, to tell the truth because a man is dead? There are times when silence may be observed; but not when truthful historic are written, and good and bad actions alike pass in review. Biographers, wishing to eulogize the heroes of whom they write, usually suppress important facts in regard to their characters, and exaggerate others, until they make demi-gods of very common personages.

It was a habit in a past age to deify all persons of distinction; and, it is said, the habit still prevails in semi-civilized China. The consequence has been that many names have come down as worthy exemplars for our imitation, who, were they living to-day, and practicing the vices and crimes they were hourly perpetrating, we would lose no time in closing the bars of a penitentiary on them, else execute them on the gallows.

Many of our modern histories are only fictions of an idle brain. The authors clothe their characters in habiliments of perfection, yea, of god, and genuine merit is left to languish and die in obscurity.

The writer bows to no shrine but Truth. He has seen too many heroes manufactured from very poor material to have an excess of love for any of them. The best of characters had their frailties. These must be known, to judge correctly of their worth.

If professed historians and biographers overdo their characters, it is due the living that their falsehoods be corrected, and their concealments exposed to the full light of day.

In writing of John Brown and Jas. H. Lane, for preservation by the Historical Society of Kansas, as before stated, I shall endeavor to give the truth as I saw it. If these facts add additional lustre to their fame, it is well; if they detract therefrom it is the misfortune of the characters that they were human, not gods, as their biographers, eulogists and romancers would have us believe.

Inviting impartial criticism to everything herein said, we submit the whole to the candid consideration of a truth-loving public.

Reminiscences of Old John Brown.

THRILLING INCIDENTS OF BORDER LIFE IN KANSAS.

FIRST NOTICE OF JOHN BROWN IN KANSAS HISTORY.

I think it was sometime in August, of 855, that the proceedings of an "Ultra Abolitionist" convention, held somewhere in Central New York, were first published in the *Anti-Slavery Standard*. The convention was presided over by the Hon. Gerritt Smith. During the first day the report, as published, stated in substance that "A gentleman standing six feet in his boots, thin face, dark complexion, with flowing beard, and gray hair, lithe and straight, about sixty years of age, arose and said: "That he had four sons in Kansas, and three others who wished to join them there, but they had not funds to pay their way; besides, he was opposed to sending any person there without arms; that he was a firm believer in the doctrine that "Without the shedding of blood there is no remission;" that if the actors in this convention were ultra abolitionists, as they claimed, and desired to do something practical for Kansas, they would arm and send his three remaining sons to Kansas, and send arms to the boys already there; that if they would do so he would accompany them, and would promise a good report of their doings."

In the proceedings of the following day appeared the statement that "Gerritt Smith presented to John Brown, in open session, seven voltaic repeaters, seven broad swords, seven muskets with bayonets, and a purse of gold; and told him to go to Kansas, take his remaining sons with him, arm them; and, as he had promised, make a faithful report of his action there in behalf of human freedom, and in the cause of the oppressed."

More than twenty-four years lie between the reading of those proceedings and the present; but the main facts are indelibly enstamped on my memory, and why?

My father had a brother by the name of John Brown. He removed to Western New York, sometime between 1810 and 1815. The last heard of him he was a Sheriff in some western county. In arresting a prisoner he received a pistol shot in his body, and his physician wrote the family he would probably die. When I read these proceedings I thought t possible the earnest John Brown was the living uncle, and more particularly as his age, size, &c., generally coincided with that of my lost relative, of whom I had often heard my father speak.

ACQUAINTANCE OF THE SONS.

The Big Springs Convention, where the Free State party was organized, was convened on the 5th of September, 1855. I was a delegate, and I think one of the secretaries. In reading the list of delegates, reported by the committee on credentials, the names of John Brown, Jr. and Frederick Brown, occurred as in attendance from Pottawattomie Creek. I saw who answered to the name when called, and, at my first leisure, made my way to John, Jr., and inquired if he was one of the sons of John Brown, the actor in the recent Abolition Convention of New York. He answered in the affirmative. I introduced myself, had but a few words of hasty conversation, and found that our families were in no way connected. He introduced me to his brother Frederick. During recess we had further conversation, and at the close of the convention they accompanied me to Lawrence, and remained at my home over night.

Another Free State Convention was held at Topeka, on the 19th and 20th of October, 1855, where I again met the brothers John and Frederick. We stopped at the same boarding house and John and I occupied the same bed. I am thus definite that the reader may understand how and why I became so well acquainted with the character of whom I write.

THE WAKARUSA WAR.

We pass to the 27th of November, 1855, when the tocsin of war was again sounded in Lawrence.

Chas W. Dow, a former employe in the *Herald of Freedom* office, was killed by F. M. Coleman, some ten to twelve miles south of Lawrence, on the 21st of November, 1855, growing out of a dispute between the parties, relative to a division line between their respective claims. He was shot in the back, while leaving a blacksmith shop, where each of the parties had been for work. Dow was boarding with Jacob Branson, and his body was removed there. On the 26th of November, a public meeting was held by citizens of the neighborhood, and resolutions were passed resolving to bring Coleman, with his accomplices, Hargus and Buckley, to justice. On the same day of the meeting, Harrison Buckley swore out a peace warrant against Branson, and placed it in the hands of S. J. Jones, who wrote himself "Sheriff of Douglas county," for execution.

Branson's residence was broken into by a force estimated at twenty-five, on the night of the 26th, and he was taken by a circuitous route to the crossing of the Wakarusa, at Blanton's Bridge, near which he was rescued by his neighbors, under the command of S. N. Wood, of Lawrence, who had been in the neighborhood of the excitement during the day.

Jones, who, though "Sheriff of Douglas county," Kansas, was at the same time Postmaster at Westport, Mo., sent dispatches to Missouri, and *afterwards* to Gov. Shannon, whose headquarters were at the Shawnee Mission, two miles from Westport for assistance.

A proclamation was immediately issued by that functionary, stating that Lawrence was in rebellion; demanding the people to lay down their arms, and calling upon the forces of the Territory to rally to the aid of the Sheriff, and aid in enforcing his process. Missouri, as was her habit on such occasions, responded, and an army some 2,000 strong was soon raised, and with shot guns, muskets stolen from the government arsenal at Liberty, and whatever weapons they could get hands on, with a piece of artillery, moved on the fated town.

At Lawrence we were constantly advised, by volunteer messengers, of what was transpiring. A meeting of the citizens was hastily called, and the facts were stated. We knew that Missouri only wanted a pretext for our entire extinction. A Committee of Public Safety was immediately appointed, consisting of ten persons, of which I had the honor of being a member. I was also a member of the Territorial Executive Committee, as before stated, appointed at Big Springs on the fifth of September, re-indorsed at the Topeka Convention on the 19th of September, and confirmed by the Constitutional Convention in October, and by a provision in the Constitution itself. The Lawrence meeting closed with the appointment of that Committee of Public Safety, which was clothed with ample power for the emergency. The Committee held an immediate session, organized by the election of a Chairman and Secretary. On my motion Dr. Chas. Robinson was made Commander-in-Chief, and was empowered to appoint subordinates, to organize the forces of the town, and do whatever was necessary for the common defense; he to report his action to the Committee for approval. Provision was made that a quorum of the Committee, consisting of six members at least, should continue in session until the impending danger should pass. Their headquarters, as that of the Commander and his subordinates, were in the Free State Hotel, whilst the Territorial Executive Committee held its sessions at the office of John Hutchinson and A. D. Searl, on the East side of the street Being a member of each Committee, my presence during the day was almost continually required with one or the other.

Moments of leisure were filled in writing a daily journal of the incidents of the campaign, which was published in the next number of the *Herald of Freedom* after the close of the war, while nights I did service on picket.

The Commander dispatched messengers to various Free State settlements asking assistance. These requests were promptly responded to, as all were aware the common fate would be that of Lawrence, until some 800 persons had assembled, with such rude arms as they could command for defense. Defenses were thrown up, sentinels were posted, and everything put on a war-like appearance.

JOHN BROWN IN LAWRENCE.

It was near sunset, I should think about the 3rd of December, when, in the distance, towards the South, a strange looking object was seen approaching Lawrence. With many others I watched it. As it neared it proved to be the skeleton of a horse, covered with a poorly-stuffed skin, wearily dragging a rather large one-horse lumber wagon. I think there were seven men standing in the box, which was made of wide, undressed, and weather-stained boards. Each man supported himself by a pole, of probably six to eight feet in length, surmounted with a bayonet. The poles were upright, and held in place at the sides of the box by leather loops nailed to the sides. Each man had a voltaic repeater strapped to his person, as also a short navy sword; at the same time supporting a musket at the position of "order." A formidable arsenal, well manned—all but the horse.

As the party dismounted I grasped the hands of John and Frederick Brown, who introduced me to their father and brothers. Leaving the horse unhitched at the door I took the whole family to the rooms of the Committee of Public Safety, and introduced them. On my suggestion a company of veterans was soon organized and the command given to Old John Brown, who he represented had served as a private at the battle of Plattsburg, in the war of 1812. [If this is true, he was but fourteen years of age, as we see by his life he was born May 2, 1800. The battle of Plattsburg was fought in Sept. 1814.] My father, who held a Captain's commission in that war, and was an active participant in the battle there, was made 1st Lieutenant, and I think O. Wilmarth was 2d Lieutenant. The whole company, as thus organized, consisted of twenty-five members. Here, at my suggestion, John Brown was first clothed with the title of Captain, conferred on him in the Wakarusa war, by Gov. Robinson, and approved by the Committee of Public Safety.

On the 9th of December an understanding was reached between Gov. Shannon, representing the beleagures, Gov. Robinson and Col. Lane, representing the citizens.

On the 10th the people were marshalled in front of the Free State Hotel, from the steps of which Gov. Shannon made a short speech, in which he stated that matters had been unfortunately precipitated by their not understanding each other, and that he was glad to have a pacific termination of the affair. I think Gov. Robinson made a few remarks in the same direction. It was at this stage of procedure, when old John Brown mounted a piece of timber lying near the corner of the hotel, and began to harangue the crowd. He said the people of Missouri had come to Kansas to destroy Lawrence; that they had beleagured the town for two weeks, threatening its destruction; that they came for blood; that he believed, "Without the shedding of blood there is no remission;" and asked for volunteers to go under his command, and attack the pro-slavery camp stationed near Franklin, some four miles from Lawrence.

Listening to his speech to this point I made my way to the room of the Committee of Public Safety, where others came immediately, leaving the Captain trying to excite insubordination. Col. G. W. Smith was instructed by the Committee to place him under arrest, and detain him in custody until the excitement should cease. Col. Smith made his way direct to the Captain, took him by the arm, and requested to speak with him. Leading the Captain away, the storm that he was i citing was soon at an end.

Gov. Shannon issued orders sending his *posse* back to their homes. That night, the 14th of December a "Norther" broke upon their camp, the coldest I ever recollect in Kansas, when the beseigers, under duplicate orders—Gov. Shannon and a frigid north—made a hasty and bloodless retreat to Missouri. Capt. Brown, his sons with their military supplies, the over-burdened wagon, and the venerable horse also retired from their first field of glory.

Redpath says, page 88 of his Life of Brown, that

"He went out once with a dozen men to meet the Missouri invaders 'to draw a little blood,' as he styled it—but, at the earnest entreaties of Gen. Lane, he returned to town without doing it."

"Lane sent for him to attend a council of war. The reply was characteristic of the brave old man, who despised all manner of assumptions, with no fact behind them to give them vitality, and a title to respect."

"'Tell the General,' he said, 'that when he wants me to fight, to say so; but that is the only order I will ever obey.'"

If Redpath's assertions are true, that the Captain "despised all manner of assumption with no facts behind to give them vitality," he would have been terribly disgusted with that statement, as with nearly the entire mass of simila ones made in that eulogy of John Brown, erroneously called a "Life."

CAPT. CHARLIE LENHART.

These Recollections would be very incomplete without reference to Charley Lenhart, as he was a junior John Brown, minus the latter's principles and piety. Charley came to Kansas from Iowa, where he left a widowed mother, in the spring of 1855. He was then 18 to 19 years of age. He applied for a situation as typo in the *Herald of Freedom* office. I gave him a "case," and agreed to board him in my family, conditioned he could find lodging elsewhere. To this he assented, and commenced type-setting. He was a faithful worker, always at his post, but proved quite limited in experience as a practical printer. As I paid by the thousand for his labor, this did not affect me, so he continued, always the first at the case in the morning, and the last to leave at night.

Late in the autumn of '55, during a cold driving "Norther," accompanied with rain, he asked the privilege of lying on the floor in the office for the night. I thought the request a strange one, and inquired:

"Why don't you remain where you have been through the summer?" He replied—

"The roof is rather leaky," looking out at the driving storm.

"You don't mean to say that you have been sleeping out of doors through the summer?"

"Every night since I have been in your service, I have slept on the open prairie, and could do so to-night, but don't like to."

"That will not be necessary," I replied. "Had you reported the fact to me I could have made provision for you long ago."

From that time until he left my employ, Charley had a bed in doors. The colloquy explained why he had always disappeared late at night, with a blanket, and was so early at his post in the morning. Justice to Kansas climate requires me to say, that during all that season he was reposing on the lap of mother earth, with the stars to look upon, and the green grass a pillow, protected from the night dews by a single blanket only, he was a picture of perfect health.

Charley did faithful service for Kansas during the Wakarusa war, in the fall of '55, but from that forth I could not count on him with certainty. If there was any wild adventure on foot he was the leader, and away!

After the destruction of the *Herald of Freedom* office in '56, Lenhart seemed to have adopted a guerilla life, and I only heard of him through others thereafter. He appeared intimate with both Lane and Brown, and held himself ever ready to execute their wishes. His associates were of the dare-devil stripe, of which John E. Cook was a representative. He was fearless and brave, and always in sympathy with the *fighting* Free State men. Like old John, he required large "contributions" from the enemy, and disappeared with his patron saint in the autumn of 1859, since which I think there is no intelligence of him. It was reported he was shot under the walls of the prison at Charlestown, Va., wherein Brown was imprisoned, and where he was reconnoitering with a view of effecting the Captain's escape.

About 1864, a gentleman who knew Charley's mother well, in Iowa, called on me hoping to get some information in regard to him, he stating that after he left the *Herald of Freedom* office, she never heard again from him by letter.

PERSONAL TO THE WRITER.

The following facts concerning the writer, explains somewhat incidents closely connected with these Reminiscences, and seem necessary to understand what shall follow. He would be glad to keep in the back-ground, but cannot comprehend how he can give his recollection of events, in which he was an actor in common with the persons of whom he writes, without occupying a front position with them.

So many outrages had been perpetrated on property in transit up the Missouri, and at Kansas City, destined to Kansas, as also upon persons making their way to the Territory, that a public meeting was held at Lawrence, on the second floor of the Emigrant Aid Company's building, on Massachusetts street, on the evening of the 28th of March, 1856. Speeches were made, numerous instances of outrages were narrated, among others the breaking open of a box at Kansas City, containing a piano, directed to Orville C. Brown, of Osawatomie, under the pretense of its containing Sharp's rifles. Resolutions denouncing the occurrences were passed, and a committee was appointed, consisting of E. Nute, G. W. Brown, and G. W. Hutchinson, with instructions to visit St. Louis, Alton, Chicago, Cincinnati and Pittsburg, and to make all needful arrangements for the establishment of a trusty line of steamers, to leave some safe point on the Mississippi and land in Kansas.

I left home in obedience to these instructions, in advance of the other members of the committee on the 1st of April, descended the Missouri, and heard much en route of a contemplated raid on Lawrence "as soon as the grass shall grow."

At Alton I called a public meeting, and elicited great enthusiasm among business men, in the enterprise. Going to Chicago, I made arrangements in that city for a public meeting a few evenings after. My name having been published in the list of "arrivals," Jas. Redpath, being in the city, saw the notice, and called on me at the Tremont. He stated he was on his way to Kansas and wished to borrow a revolver. As the history of that revolver, which I loaned him, will form my next sub-division, I will hasten to close my own connection with these incidents by stating that soon after I visited Rockford, talked to a good audience in Warner's Hall, on the night after the municipal election, while bonfires and rejoicings were going on outside over the election of Jas. L. Loop as Mayor. Thence I started for Chicago to fill my engagements there; was taken with a congestive chill in the cars, and was almost death sick all day. Again stopped at the Tremont, was carried almost by force from my sick bed to Market Hall, [was it?] where I was requested to "show" myself, but at which, in addition, with a raging fever, I spoke over an hour on Kansas matters, and of the causes of a movement for a direct line of steamers to that Territory. What I said, or how I said it, I never had any recollection, for I was suffering too much physically to hardly know anything. The next day I took passage for the Lake View Water Cure, where I remained five days. When sufficiently recovered to journey, I returned to Chicago, and was about starting for Cincinnati, when my eye fell upon a telegram in the *Democratic Press*, bringing intelligence of the shooting at Lawrence of "S. J. Jones, Sheriff of Douglas county." I changed my direction, went to Alton; thence to St. Louis; chartered a steamer at my own risk; and returned with it to Alton, where I received a party of about one hundred Michigan pioneers, on their way to Kansas, under the direction of Rev. A. St. Clair; thence up the river; at Lexington learned of the arrest, by a mob, of Gov. Robinson at that place the day previous; on to Kansas City; besieged a couple of days by a mob which surrounded the hotel, but did not enter; thence started at night with Gaius Jenkins for Lawrence; both captured in going half a mile; taken to the Harris House, at Westport, Mo., prisoners; an *ex parte* trial for our lives by the ruffians, who finally sent us to the Territory under Henry Clay Pate, I arriving at Lecompton on the 20th of May, the day before the destruction of Lawrence by the semi-legal mob. This much, hurriedly, for myself, to make what shall follow better understood.

HISTORY OF A REVOLVER.

Mr. Redpath was instructed, on his arrival in Lawrence, to leave the revolver mentioned above, which was an Allen patent, known as a "pepper box," on the border, with Miss Aunis W. Gleason, the clerk in the *Herald of Freedom* office. He did so.

About this time a new attempt was set on foot to arrest S. N. Wood, for the rescue of Branson, in the autumn previous. The "grass had begun to grow," and the threats I heard when descending the Missouri were about to be executed.

"Sheriff Jones," with a *posse* of United States troops, entered Lawrence, and camped on the night of the 23d of April in canvas tents, a little North-east of the *Herald of Freedom* building, on some open lots.

Early in the evening Charley Lenhart called on Miss Gleason, and asked for the loan of a revolver. The one returned by Redpath, mentioned above, was passed to him, with no idea, on her part, of the uses he desired to put it to. He examined the weapon, saw it was fully loaded; went in the direction of Jones' camp; was gone but a few minutes, when Miss G. heard the discharge of a revolver, and soon Charley came running back to the office. He passed her the wicked instrument, one barrel of which was discharged. She put it away, and learned almost immediately thereafter of the shooting of "Sheriff Jones," *the first blood actually drawn by Free Soil men* in Kansas, and which transaction was deeply regretted by every sincere friend of the Free State cause. A public meeting of the citizens was held the next morning denouncing the event, and a reward of $500 was offered by Gov. Robinson, for the arrest and conviction of the offender in the United States District Court. Charley was strongly suspected of knowing something of the matter; but this is probably the first published account of it. He has long been beyond the reach of those who would punish him, and now I only give it publicity, that the praise or censure may fall where it rightfully belongs.

Jones recovered from his injury, and on the 21st of the following month, made the people of Lawrence realize, as I experienced to my own sorrow, with many others, the truth of the following quotation from Byron's Mazeppa:

> There never yet was human power,
> Which could evade, if unforgiven,
> The patient search and vigil long
> Of him who treasures up a wrong!

Three other exciting incidents were connected with that revolver, either of which would form a valuable chapter in a "blood and thunder novel." The following, being historic, will conclude its story; anticipating somewhat the order of events:—

Dr. John Doy was captured in Missouri, charged with aiding in the escape of slaves. He was taken to St. Joseph, Mo., and imprisoned in the county jail, awaiting trial. During that period, the writer, was called upon for the loan of a revolver. It was passed to the party. A few days later news came of the breaking of the jail at St. Jo., on the night of the 23d of July, 1859; the rescue of Doctor D.; and, soon after, was informed of the transactions by one of the actors, of which I had no previous intimation, and of the loss overboard, while crossing the river in the darkness of night, of the identical weapon fired by Lenhart, at "Sheriff Jones." Had Jones died, and the ancient English law of *deodand* been still in force, that revolver could not now be taken for "pious uses." It reposes beneath the turbid waves of the Missouri.

SACKING OF LAWRENCE – ARREST OF FREE STATE PRISONERS.

On the 21st of May, 1856, Lawrence was sacked, as before stated, by a pro-slavery mob, called together by United States Marshal Donaldson. His posse, as he called them, were then disbanded, and passed over to Sheriff Jones, who had mostly recovered from the effects of Charley Lenhart's bullet. The Free State Hotel was demolished. It was a fine stone structure, fully completed and furnished, and was opened on that very day, under the auspices of S. W. Eldridge, to the public. The residence of Gov. Robinson was burned, with his furniture and fine library. The *Herald of Freedom* office was destroyed, its types were thrown into the river, its two hand presses, and a small cylinder fast running Taylor Power Press, were broken, and a large library and heavy stock of paper were cut to pieces or carried away. The *Free State* office and entire contents met a similar fate. The town was overrun and pillaged by the lawless invaders. They were not resisted, because the Marshal had come under the pretext of executing legal process from a United States Court. It was well known that this was a plan of the pro-slavery leaders, hoping to bring on a collision between the Free State people and the federal government. They had already, before a packed Grand Jury, made up of South Carolinians, Missourians and southerners, all but a few days in the Territory, procured indictments for *high treason* against A. H.

Reeder, Chas. Robinson, G. W. Brown, G. W. Smith, G. W. Deitzler, and Samuel C. Pomeroy. The latter's name was erased, and the name of Gaius Jenkins was interlined. This was done long after the Grand Jury adjourned.

Gov. Robinson had been captured by a mob at Lexington, Mo., nine days before, while with his wife going down the Missouri; G. W. Brown was captured on the 14th of May, by residents of Missouri, without legal process, in Kansas City, while making his way to Lawrence. He reached Lecompton on the 20th, Mr. Jenkins being with him when arrested, but was discharged on the evening of the 19th, and re-arrested on the 21st, with Judge Smith and Col. Deitzler, all of whom were placed under guard in the same room with myself, at Lecompton. Gov. Robinson was started for the Territory, and reached Franklin, within four miles of Lawrence. His captors, fearing a rescue, took him back to Kansas City thence to Leavenworth, where he arrived on the 24th of May.

Mention is made of these facts that the reader may keep connectedly in mind the general condition of affairs at the period referred to; without any intention of entering into details.

HORRIBLE MURDERS ON THE POTTAWOTOMIE.

On Sunday, late in the afternoon of the 25th of May, '56, information was given to the treason prisoners, at Lecompton, of which the writer had the honor of being one, that a terrible massacre of pro-slavery men had been perpetrated on Pottawotomie creek; that the news had reached the Kickapoo Rangers, Atchison Tigers, and such other pro-slavery organizations as were still about Lecompton, after their successful raid of the 21st on Lawrence. The excitement was reported very high among them.

On the evening of the 25th Marshal Donaldson entered the building in person, and said that a party were organizing among the Rangers, Tigers, &c., to take the prisoners and hang them in retaliation for these murders. He said he had learned that we were all Odd Fellows or Masons; that he had so reported; and besides enlisting all the Territorial officers, including the Governor, Judges, &c., and such members of the Orders as he could find in Lecompton, he had found some in the several companies, and with these he hoped to be able to save us; that they should stand guard through the night, and if an attack was made he should place arms in our hands, that we might aid in our own defense.

The guard was kept up for the night. The next day the Marshal's "posse" were again discharged, and left Lecompton; but Donaldson himself remained with us in the room for the night, for our protection against contingencies, as he asserted.

DETAILS OF THE MASSACRE.

My pen is not capable of describing the horrors of that event. Death by the hand of violence is always terrible; committed at the hour of midnight, adds additional terrors to it; but when the bodies are fiendishly mutilated, with awful imprecations on the authors of such transactions, we recall to memory the most sanguinary deeds of American savages. The murderer, stimulated to crime by passion, or led on by hopes of gain, may, under some circumstances, arrest our sympathy; but he who mutilates the dead body of his victim, whether a Col. Chivington, or his command, revelling in the blood of his victim; a Modoc chieftan, taking vengeance on an enemy, or the Inquisition, with rack and torture, tearing limb from limb from the writhing and dying heretic, must only excite our abhorrence.

We charge no one with these outrages upon humanity. Our province is to state the facts, and leave the reader, or the historian, to make his own deductions.

That five persons were killed, in the neighborhood of the Pottowatomie, some time towards the last of May, 1856, is not susceptible of a doubt. The sworn evidence of several witnesses fixes the time as the morning of the 25th of May, but other facts fix the time as late on the night of the 23d, and the morning of the 24th, and I am inclined to adopt the latter dates. No person has ever denied the murders, and the exact date is not necessary. These men were taken from their homes during the darkness of night, one from the bed of a sick wife, unable to help herself, and was found the next morning "about one hundred and fifty yards from the house, in some dead brush," * * with "a gash in his head and side, * * and his throat cut twice." Another was found in a creek near his residence. His "skull was split open in two places, and some of his brains were washed out by the water. A large hole was cut in his breast, and his left hand was cut off, except a little piece of skin on one side."

A father and two sons, additional to the above, were massacred, and found "about one hundred and fifty yards from the house, in the grass, near a ravine." The "father was shot in the forehead and stabbed in the breast." One of the son's "head was cut open, and a hole was made in his jaw, as though it was made by a knife, and a hole also in his side." Another son was found with his "fingers cut off, and his arms were cut off; his head was cut open; there was a hole in his breast."

The above passages, in quotation, are copied verbatim from affidavits made by witnesses who saw the terrible sight; who swore to the statements before legal authority; it was published soon after; was accessible to everybody; and yet, so far as we know, there has never been a denial of the killing, or of the mutilation by any party who was trying to tell the truth.

Wm. A. Phillips, a sensational correspondent of the New York *Tribune*, who published in 1856, a volume of 414 pages, entitled "The Conquest of Kansas," page 316, writing of this tragedy, says: "It was one of those stern and remorseless acts in civil war which make the delicate and sensitive shrink." This work was published as a campaign document, in the presidential election of that year, in the interest of his party. While he did not deny the murders he does say: "The frightful stories about mutilation were unfounded, as applied to this affair. A Mr. Sherman, WHO WAS KILLED AT THAT TIME, was killed by the Camanches, he having gone out to the plains to hunt Buffalo. The Indians not only killed him, but mutilated his body; and his friends when they found his body, brought it home to Pottowatomie. The pro-slavery men in the neighborhood took advantage of this circumstance to confound this affair with the other, and charge it upon the abolitionists! and it afforded a fine theme for war extras along the Missouri frontier. *Free State men, too, believing the worst pro-slavery version of it, held meetings and denounced it.*"

I cannot believe that Mr. Phillips ever wrote that part of the above which charges the offense upon the Camanches. It is an interpolation, and a libel upon these savages, put in by the publishers, to avoid responsibility by Free State men for such a terrible affair. This is evidenced by the awkwardness of the language, which is unlike Mr. Phillips' round, easy style; besides, the killing is described as occurring *at the time* these other men were slaughtered. And yet we must hold Mr. Phillips responsible for the statement, as he has ne er denied its paternity, and it is in a book claimed to be written by him.

Such "savage barbarity and demoniac cruelty," as a prominent politician sa d of the event, practiced not only on Wm. Sherman, but on Allen Wilkenson, Jas. P. Doyle, Drury Doyle and Wm. Doyle, are certainly characteristic of North American savages; and I honor the author for his attempt, feeble as it was, to throw the responsibility for one of these cases of mutilation on one of the most violent tribes of the plains; but I have quoted in confirmation of the mutilation of these men, from affidavits made before a member of the Kansas Investigating Committee, appointed by resolution of Congress to inquire into all our Kansas troubles. These affidavits will be found, spread at length on pages 1,193, 94, 95, 96, 97, 98 and 99, of their official report made to Congress, 20,000 extra copies of which were printed and scattered over the country. The huge volume of over 1,200 pages is open before me as I write, and from which I shall have occasion again to make extracts, in endeavoring to find who these murderers and mutilating *Camanches* were! Would to heaven the truth of history would permit me to throw the veil of darkness over this awful tragedy, and allow the world to believe that not only Wm. Sherman, but his associates in death and mutilation on that fearful night died by the hands of Camanches! But we must seek elsewhere for the real murderers.

INCIDENTS OF HISTORY.

To learn the truth in regard to this tragedy, let us hurriedly state a few facts that followed the sacking of Lawrence, on the 21st of May, three or four days before the massacre. News had gone out from Lawrence, into all the Free

State settlements, of the assembling of large bodies of pro-slavery men around that ill-fated town. The whole South seemed pouring her swarms of idle and dissolute population into Kansas. Col. Buford was there with his South Carolinian followers; Col. Titus was there with his Florida cohorts; Col. Bell was there with his "fillibusters" indiscriminately raised in the South; the two Stringfellows were there with their Missouri rabble; and all were working in harmony under the lead of that master demagogue, Dave Atchison, who furnished brains for the whole.

The Free State men had witnessed the invasion of Kansas, on the 29th of November, 1854, at the first election for a delegate to Congress, when they poured over from Missouri, took possession of the polls, and cast their votes for Gen. Whitfield, excluding the Free State settlers almost wholly from participation in the election.

They saw this again on the 30th of March, 1855, at the election of members of the Legislative Assembly, when the invaders came by thousands, overran every election precinct but one in the Territory, excluded the legally appointed judges of election, placed their servile tools in their places, driving away the legal voters, and elected some of their own numbers to make laws for the residents.

The people saw these invaders again, in session at Pawnee; thence adjourned to the Shawnee Mission, a locality positively "excepted out of, and made no part of the Territory of Kansas," by provision of the organic act, which excluded Indian Territory and reservations from operation of the law; they saw them enacting a code in keeping with their character as invaders of a neighboring territory over which they had no political rights whatever.

In the autumn of 1855 they beheld an army of 2,000, thoroughly organized, officered, armed and provisioned, marching on Lawrence, breathing words of slaughter and demolition. The people had then rallied from all quarters, and stood with the residents, determined to sell their lives as dearly as possible in defense of that town.

And, now, they saw it again menaced by thousands, gathered from every Southern State, hurling imprecations against the Free State settlers, threatening to "wipe out every Northern pioneer," and divide his possessions among themselves. For days they saw Lawrence completely surrounded by this invading army, while several of their compeers, C. Robinson, G. W. Brown, J. P. Root, and others, were prisoners in their hands, and their lives were threatened.

John Brown, Jr., on the Pottawotomie, rallied his neighbors and acquaintances, and joined them with others from Osawatomie, and marched to the rescue of their friends. He had a force variously stated, ranging in number from 60 to 120. On Thursday, the 22d of May, they reached Palmyra, within twelve miles of Lawrence. They there learned of the sacking of the town; the destruction of the hotel, and printing offices, the burning of Dr. Robinson's residence; the general pillage; and the arrest of G. W. Smith, G. W. Deitzler, and Gaius Jenkins; of their removal to Lecompton, held under an indictment for *high treason !*

After reconnoitering in the vicinity for a time, they retraced their steps for a short distance, and camped for the night. On the 23d they resumed their homeward journey, and reached the vicinity of Pottawotomie, where they again encamped.

With incidents narrated to me by an eye witness, still living, and a resident of Lawrence, Kansas, whose veracity was never called in question, and whose unsupported statements would outweigh, in any court of justice acquainted with his character, the sworn statement of a hundred letter-writers, and a quotation from Redpath, I close this subdivision. My informant said:

"During the evening Old John Brown, who had accompanied the expedition to Palmyra, and returned with it to the neighborhood of the Pottawotomie, asked the attention of the men, and said he had an expedition in view, which required the assistance of some brave, bold men; that John, Jr., protested against any persons leaving the camp that night; that notwithstanding this Old John Brown and seven others left camp, armed to the teeth, and marched towards the settlements on the Pottawotomie; that they returned early the next morning; that when our informant left his tent in the morning he saw a navy sword, worn away by one of Old John Brown's recruits the night before, standing near the door of a tent, with dried blood and red hair upon it; that it was laughingly remarked that the party "must have killed a dog the night before;" that soon after the camp was rallied, when a messenger came in and reported the killing and mutilation of five men on the Pottowatomie during the night previous; that John, Jr., was greatly excited, disbanded his men and rode hurredly towards Ossawatomie."

In Redpath's Life of John Brown, page 117, I find this statement confirmed in these words:

"On the 23d of May, John Brown left the camp of his son, at Osawatomie, with seven or eight men, and from that moment began his guerilla warfare in Southern Kansas."

WHO WAS RESPONSIBLE FOR THIS MASSACRE?

Not until after Old John Brown's arrest for murder and inciting slaves to insurrection, at Harper's Ferry, on the 20th of October, 1859, two years and five months after the massacre, did I hear but one expression in Kansas, as to the party responsible for that transaction.

Pro-slavery men, as well as Free State men, accredited the affair to him. And on the very day, if I remember correctly, of his execution, a body of his friends in public convention in Lawrence, while expressing sympathy for his fate, apologized, by public resolution, for these murders. His most ardent admirers had not face to stand up before a Kansas audience, where the whole facts were so well known, and attempt a denial of his responsibility. It was left to his eastern apologists, first, to deny his connection with the affair; second, to justify the outrage on humanity, under pleas as false and specious as the crimes were abhorrent. John Brown on several occasions, once while a prisoner at Charlestown, Va., said he did not do the killing, but that he approved of it. We do not assert that his own hand struck the blow, neither did John Calvin, with his own hands, set fire to the faggots which burned Michael Servetus for heresy, but the historian holds Calvin responsible.

Brown's denial was always guarded in expression, and the reader, knowing the facts, saw there was something behind which was not fully told. In a speech made by him at Cleveland, Ohio, on the 22d of March, 1859, reported by Kagi, his Secretary of War, killed at Harper's Ferry, and published in Redpath's Life of Brown, page 239, is probably found the key to this "mental reservation.' He said, according to the report:

"He had never killed anybody; although on some occasions, he had shown the young men with him how some things might be done as well as others; *and they had done the business.*"

What "business" had the young men done? Why, the killing, which he had instructed them how to do.

On page 112 of Redpath's Life, after detailing the author's adventures "a few days after the sacking of

Lawrence," in his "first journey South," page 106, he mentions that "a Southern squatter from Pottawotomie had arrived at Lecompton with dispatches for the Governor, which announced that five pro-slavery settlers had been murdered, at midnight, and their bodies shockingly disfigured and mutilated, by a party of Free State men. He brought a request for a body of troops to protect the pro-slavery people there," &c. He then states that the troops passed through Lawrence *en route* for Osawotomie, as it was understood, to arrest John Brown, Jr., and the force he commanded. He left Lawrence to inform the Browns of their danger; recites his adventures, and on page 112, as he neared the camp of those he sought, he was interrupted by Frederick Brown, with the command, "Halt!" His recognition, and the young man's movements on the occasion, are thus narrated:

"He talked wildly, as he walked before me, turning round every minute, as he spoke of the recent affair at Pottawotomie. His family, he said, had been accused of it; he denied it indignantly, with the wild air of a maniac. His excitement was so great that he repeatedly recrossed the creek, until, getting anxious to reach the camp, I refused to listen to him until he took me to his father. He then quietly filled his pail with water, and, after many strange turnings, led me into camp."

Redpath then relates the incidents on reaching camp, and, on page 113, continues:

"Old Brown himself stood near the fire. The old man received me with great cordiality, and the little band gathered about me. But it was for a moment only, for the Captain ordered them to renew their work. *He respectfully but firmly forbade conversation on the Pottawotomie affair;* and said that if I desired any information from the company in relation to their conduct or intentions, he, as their Captain, would answer for them, whatever was proper to communicate."

This was but two to three days after the massacre, while the letter-writers were gathering material for the Eastern press, Redpath being one of them, and fully in sympathy, as we shall see further on, with a movement to bring on a "revolution."

FURTHER, WHO WAS RESPONSIBLE?

The reader may weary with these details of facts, cumulative in their character, connecting Capt. Brown with this massacre on the Pottawotomie; but it will be remembered that twenty years ago he was, through the public press, charged with it. His friends, *outside of Kansas*, denied his guilt, and he equivocated when interrogated in regard to it, by saying, "*I never shed the blood of a fellow man, except in self-defence, or in promotion of a righteous cause.*" See Redpath's Life, page 383.

F. B. Sanborn, of Concord, N. H., who is the author of the "Memoirs of John Brown," in a letter, written Nov. 26, 1878, and published in the Springfield *Republican*, used this language in regard to that event:

"That Brown was connected with this affair, and approved of it I have never doubted—that he was actually present, he always denied to me—and I shall believe him until some eye witness proves to the contrary. One eye witness has told two contradictory stories about it; and *nobody has yet made public the whole truth,*"

Though the writer was not an "eye-witness," yet he believes he is in possession of the whole "truth," and it is with an earnest desire to reach that point that he continues these inquiries. The "eye-witnesses" were accomplices in the transaction, and it is safe to expect from them "contradictory stories." Before the evidence is finally closed, his friends will withdraw their attempt to prove an *alibi*, and rely upon *justifying*, else set up the plea of *insanity*, which Brown rejected with so much scorn at Harper's Ferry. We continue:

Mrs. Robinson, in her "Kansas, Its Interior and Exterior," written in "Camp near Lecompton," where her husband and the other Free State prisoners were held for *high treason*, guarded by a regiment of United States troops, as she could not, even as a partisan of the times, vindicate the transaction, very properly passed it over, merely telling her readers of the inflammatory statements which were spread along the Missouri border in consequence; and then she describes somewhat in the order of their occurrence the events following, and growing directly out of these murders.

Phillips, in his "Conquest of Kansas," seems horrified on account of these murders, and says:

"A party of seven or eight guerillas, NOT YOUNG MEN, BUT STERN DETERMINED MEN, attacked them, and in the scuffle every pro-slavery man was killed."

Redpath, page 99, aids us somewhat in finding out who these "guerillas, not young men, but stern determined men," were, in the following words:

"John Brown, Jr, marched back to Osawatomie [from Palmyra,] but ere he reached it and disbanded *his father*, with a company of seven men, left his camp, and began in right earnest the war of liberty."

Mr. Phillips well knew that these men were not killed in a body; that they were taken from their homes during the darkness of night, and one by one were murdered and mutilated, and Redpath calls it the beginning of "The War of Liberty." A few lines further down the page Phillips says: "It was one of those cases at which enlightened humanity will shudder." He denies the mutilation, and then invents the tale of Sherman being killed and mutilated by Camanches!

Redpath, who always justified and encouraged the shedding of blood; who, in his "Roving Editor," says he "went to Kansas to incite a revolution," and whose every action, by pen and otherwise, was in that direction, falsely ascribes the provocation to a state of facts that did not exist, then justified the killing, but denies the participation of old John Brown in it, though he informs us that the Captain "*approved of it.*"

John Doyle, a son of the murdered man, and brother of Drury and William Doyle, who gave testimony to the Congressional Investigating Committee, previously referred to, in an affidavit dated June 6th, 1856, only a few days after the murder, says:

"An old man commanded the party: he was dark complected, and his face was thin. We had lighted a candle, and *about eight of them entered the house*; there were some more outside."

James Harris, also an Investigating Committee witness, says he was living in Sherman's house, in bed with his own wife and child, when

"We were aroused by a company of men who said they belonged to the Northern army, and who were each armed with a sabre and two revolvers; two of them I recognized, namely: a Mr. Brown, whose given name I do not remember, commonly known by the appellation of 'Old Man Brown,' and his son Owen.   *   *   Old Mr. Brown and his son went into the house with me.   *   *   Brown asked Mr. Sherman to go out with him, and Mr. Sherman then went out with old Mr. Brown, and another came into the house in Brown's place. I heard nothing more for about 15 minutes. Two of the Northern Army, as they styled themselves, stayed in with us until we heard a cap burst, and then these two men left. That morning about ten o'clock I found Wm. Sherman dead in the creek near my house."

The above is followed with a description by the witness of the mutilation, copied further back. Phillips says he was killed and mutilated by Camanches! How much short does this evidence fall of the "eye-witness" desired by Sanborn, and what other proof is required to associate the "father of Owen Brown" with the Camanches?

Mrs. Wilkinson, in her affidavit to the Investigating Committee, made on the 13th of June, 1856, less than three weeks after the murder, said:—

"I believe that one of Capt. Brown's sons was in the party who murdered my husband; I heard a voice like his. I do not know Capt. Brown himself. * * The old man who seemed to be the commander wore soiled clothes, and a straw hat pulled down over his face. He spoke quick; is a tall, narrow-faced, elderly man."

Morrow B. Lowry, of Erie, Pa., a personal friend of the writer, visited John Brown while in prison at Charlestown, and, referring to this affair, "ventured the remark that his reputation demanded an explanation." Brown replied: "Time and the honest verdict of posterity will approve of every act of mine to prevent slavery from being established in Kansas. I never shed the blood of a fellow-man, except in self-defense or in promotion of a righteous cause."

Here is no denial of the killing; no claim by the man himself of an *alibi;* but a firm reliance on "posterity" for justification.

NEWLY DISCOVERED EVIDENCE.

I might close the testimony at this point, and submit the case, as to the connection of Capt. Brown with this Pottawotomie affair, to the impartial verdict of the reader; but I have before me the letter referred to above, written to the Springfield *Republican* touching this subject. I will give it in Mr. Sanborn's own words, punctuation and parenthesis. It will be seen it corroborates to the letter and date, every assertion we have previously made on this subject, and, what is strange, on the hypothesis that Brown was not immediately connected with it, while he mentions that he is charged with guilt, he only retorts by criminating his friends at Osawotomie and Lawrence, designating their refusal to fight the United States troops as "cowardly" and "mean." I quote from Sanborn's letter; the italics are mine:

"I have before me a letter of John Brown's, never yet printed. * * He says: "We were called to the relief of Lawrence, May 22, and every man, (eight in all) except Orson turned out; he staying with the women and children, and to take care of the cattle. John (Jr.) was captain of a company to which Jackson belonged. The other six were a little company by ourselves. On our way to Lawrence we learned that it had been already destroyed, and we encamped with John's company over night. (This must have been the night of May 22, Thursday.) Next day our little company left, and during the day we stopped and searched three men. On the second day and evening after we left John's men; ("this was Saturday, May 24, and on that evening the Pottawotomie ruffians were shot,") *we encountered quite a number of pro slavery men* and took quite a number prisoners. Our prisoners we let go, but we kept some four or five horses. *We were immediately after this accused of murdering five men at Pottawotomie, and great efforts have since been made by the Missourian's and others, ruffian allies, to capture us.* John's company soon afterwards disbanded, and also the Osawotomie men. John tried to hide for several days, but from the feelings of the ungrateful conduct of those who had ought to have stood by him, excessive fatigue, anxiety and loss of sleep, became quite *insane,* and in that condition gave up, or, as we are told, was betrayed at Osawotomie into the hands of the Bogus men. We do not know all the truth about this affair. The *cowardly mean* conduct of Osawotomie and vicinity did not save them, for the ruffians came on them, made numerous prisoners, fired their buildings and robbed them. It is said that both the Lawrence and Osawatomie men, when the ruffians came on them, either hid or gave up their arms, and that their leading men counseled, to take such a course? "This letter bears date, near Osawatomie," June 24, 1856."

So much for the letter and Sanborn's interpolations in brackets. It was written from "near Osawatomie," which was about seven miles from the scene of this massacre, just one month to a day, after the murder. Under another head I shall have occasion to refer to this letter again

THE CAMANCHES DISCOVERED.

I find in the "First Biennial Report of the State Board of Agriculture for Kansas," Vol. 6, published in 1878, under the head of Miami County, page 311, the following very clear, but in some respects inaccurate, account of this transaction. from the pen of E. W. Robinson, Esq., long a resident of the county, located at Paola, but a few miles distant. His veracity no man will call in question. He says:

"On the 24th of May, Winans, a Free State man, who kept a store on Mosquito Creek, brought the intelligence to the Free State camp, near Ottawa, commonly called 'Toywa Jones,' that the anti-slavery settlers on the Pottawotomie had been ordered to leave. On the reception of this news a detachment, under command of John Brown, Sr., at once set out, on the evening of the 24th, for the relief and protection of the settlers.

"On arriving at the residence of Mr. Doyle, on Mosquito Creek, near the mouth of the Pottawotomie, the party stopped and called Doyle out, and when he appeared they fell on him with heavy cutlasses and sabres, and hacked him to death. Doyle's two sons, coming to the rescue of their father, met with a similar fate.

"From Doyle's the party proceeded to the house of Allen Wilkinson, who was especially obnoxious, on account of his having been a member of the 'Bogus Legislature,' and, on making his appearance, the party murdered him. A Mr. Sherman, living on the Pottawotomie, was also murdered by the same party."

This seems sufficiently definite. An active member of the Republican party, resident in the immediate vicinity of this massacre, and writing for home use, a historical sketch of his county, says John Brown, Sr., commanded the detachment. And he says they "hacked" the Doyle's to death, and "*murdered*" Wilkinson, and "*murdered*" Sherman! And he tells us in so many words, who 'Phillips' Camanches were! The writer has been careful to withhold a statement of even his *opinion* in the premises, content to collate such facts as are open to the world.

TERRIBLE ARRAIGNMENT.

The following, sent to John Brown, and read to him by the Sheriff, in prison, while the Captain was under sentence of death, is a terrible finale of that horrible massacre. Whether the "Liberator," as his friends called him, was guilty, or or otherwise, it tells in sad, sorrowful, and bitter words who the lonely wife and mother believed the murderer of her husband and sons:

"CHATTANOOGA, Tenn., Nov. 20, 1859.

JOHN BROWN—*Sir:*—Although vengeance is not mine, I confess that I do feel gratified to hear that you were stopped in your fiendish career at Harper's Ferry, with the loss of your two sons. You can now appreciate my distress in Kansas, when you then and there entered my house at midnight and arrested my husband and two boys, and took them out in the yard, and in cold blood shot them dead in my hearing. You can't say you did it to free our slaves; we had none, and never expected to own one; but it only made me a poor disconsolate widow, with helpless children. While I feel for your folly, I do hope and trust you will meet with your just reward. Oh, how it pained my heart to hear the dying groans of my husband and children. If this scrawl gives you any satisfaction, you are welcome to it.

MAHALA DOYLE.

"N. B.—My son, John Doyle, whose life I begged of you, is now grown up, and is very desirous to be at Charlestown, on the day of your execution; would certainly be there if his means would permit it, that he might adjust the rope around your neck, if Gov. Wise would permit." M. D.

Three and a half years only had passed,

at the time of writing that terribly vindicative letter, since that fatal night on the Pottawotomie, when Mrs. Doyle's husband, and sons were slain. She had left Kansas, with the remaining members of her family, the youngest only five years old, and had struggled as only a mother will, to keep them near her. No one can know the anguish of heart; the poverty; the wretchedness; the suffering which had been hers in consequence. Though the reader, I hope, similarly circumstanced, would not have written such a letter, yet, in her bereaved condition, she was human, and it tells more forcibly than words of mine to whom *she* ascribed the cause of her woe.

MOTIVE FOR THE KILLING.

The motive for the killing of these men, on the Pottawotomie, as given by various authors, are so varied and numerous it will be difficult, if not impossible, to arrive at the truth, other than by implication.

1. R. J. Hinton, a very intimate friend of Capt. Brown, who designed to have been at Harper's Ferry, but could not get away, according to Cook, one of the accomplices, in a letter of Dec. 3, '59, to the Boston *Traveler*, said:

"Doyle was engaged with others in a fiendish attempt to outrage the persons of Capt. Brown's daughter and daughter-in-law, the wife of one of Brown's sons." hence the murder.

2. J. R. Brown, a brother of old John, writing to the Cleveland *Plaindealer*, of date Nov 22, '59, says:

"My brother John and his two sons were living in the same neighborhood, and a committee of five from the Border Ruffian camp called upon him, and said that they were instructed to warn him that if the Free State men were found there the next Thursday night, they would kill every one of them."

3. A statement went through the Eastern press excusing the killing, by saying that:

"The old man was driven to violence by the murder of his son, Frederick, and the arrest of John, Jr., who was chained and driven forty miles in a hot sun, etc."

Both of these events followed, and was in consequence of these murders. John, Jr., when arrested, was suspicioned of being one of the banditti; and Frederick was killed on the morning of the 30th of August, more than three months *after* the murders, hence we must seek elsewhere for the cause.

4. Still another statement was made that—

"A band of pro-slavery men went to the house of John, Jr., insulted his wife, burned his cabin, and drove off his cattle."

The cabins of the sons of old John Brown were burned by pro-slavery men, on the 27th or 28th of May, three to four days after the massacre, and because of it.

5. "John Brown's cabin was burned, his blooded stock were driven off, and the women of his family were grossly insulted."

John Brown never had a cabin in Kansas, nor owned or exercised ownership over one foot of Kansas soil. His family, through all his western adventures, were residents of North Elba, Essex county, New York. In answer to Valandingham, while in Charlestown jail, Captain Brown said in so many words: "I did not go to Kansas to settle, but because of the difficulties."

6. "That Wilkinson, Sherman and the Doyles were caught in the act of hanging a Free State man, and were shot by friends of the injured party."

7. Old John Brown told A. E. Coleman, Esq., residing near Lawrence, Kan., that he,

'Brown, ran a survey line through each of the cabins of the murdered men, and, on account of being a stranger, heard from their own lips a plan to drive out the entire Free State settlers; that it was merely a question whether to submit to being driven out, or to drive out those who were threatening their neighbors."

This statement was made long after the event, when the transaction needed vindication.

8. Redpath's Life of John Brown, p. 113 says:

"On the night of the 25th of May, the Doyles, Wilkinson and Sherman were seized, tried and slain. This act was precipitated by a brutal assault committed during the forenoon on a Free State man, at the store of Sherman, in which the Doyles were the principal and most ruffianly participators."

9. Captain Brown in answering a question from the Chairman of the Massachusetts Legislature, in Boston, on the 18th of February, 1857, said:

"He saw a great deal of Buford's men in Kansas; that they spoke without hesitation before him, because he employed himself as a surveyor; and, as nearly all the surveyors were pro-slavery men, they probably thought he was 'sound on the goose.' They told him all their plans; what they intended to do; how they were determined to drive off the Free State men, and possess themselves of the Territory, and make it a slave State at all hazards, cost what it might. * * They did not hesitate to threaten that they would burn, kill, scalp, and drive out the entire Free State population of the Territory, if it was necessary to do so to accomplish their object."

The above was, probably, the original of the survey story, and was varied from time to time, by different reporters, to accommodate varying *circumstances*.

TOO GOOD TO MURDER.

But it is said that Old John Brown's whole character was antagonistic to such outrages upon humanity, as were these on the Pottawotomie; that he was a religious man, of Puritanic faith and practice; a praying man, and that the violent shedding of blood was not in harmony with his Christian life, his great love for the negro, and his desire for heir liberation from a life of toil and slavery. The reader will please remember his oft-quoted expression, "Without the shedding of blood there is no remission." Some of the vilest characters whose names have come down to us, have falsified the pure teachings of the Master, by an almost indiscriminate massacre of those who entertained religious convictions in opposition to them. Their faith did not save them from an exhibition of brutal sions.

Will some reader who has implicit confidence in old John Brown's piety being sufficient to shield him from such acts of violence, give interpretation to the following extract, which I make from page 191, Redpath's Life of Brown? It was while the Captain was in Boston, in the winter of 1857. Says the biographer,—the italics are mine:

"Mr. Stearns, an active and generous friend of Kansas, tells two incidents of John Brown's visit to Boston at this time, which are *exceedingly characteristic of the old Puritan:*

"Shortly after his introduction to him, Mr. Stearns said, one day, half jestingly, 'I suppose, Captain Brown, that if Judge Lecompte had fallen into your hands, he would have fared rather hard?'

"The old man turned round in his chair, and, in the most earnest tones, said, '*If the Lord had delivered Judge Lecompte into my hands, it would have required the Lord to have taken him out again!*'"

EFFECT OF THE MASSACRE ON THE FREE STATE PARTY.

Phillips' Conquest of Kansas, page 117, says:—

"The effect of this act was highly beneficial to the Free State men. * * Every one in Kansas admitted the fact, although many of them deny it now."

When did they "deny" that it was "beneficial?" Why, "*now*," when his book was published, on the first of August, 1856, two months only after the massacre. And why did "many of them deny it" so soon after the transaction? Possibly they had noticed the consequences growing out of, and directly traceable to that tragedy. Suppose, reader, we lift the veil of the past enshrouding Kansas history, and, perchance, ere we close, you, too, may be one who denies that beneficial results follow murder and mutilation? We read *somewhere* that, "He who takes the sword shall perish by the sword." There are but few who have not observed that "violence begets violence."

Mrs. Robinson was on the Missouri at the time of this occurrence. She says page 273, of her "Kansas Interior and Exterior."

"The last day or two of the trip on the Missouri river, rumors of war became more frequent. Inflammatory extras were thrown upon the boats at different landings. * * The extras stated the murder of eight pro-slavery men by the abolitionists, and the cruel mutilation of their bodies."

I have already stated how the news of these murders was received in Lecompton, and the determination to retaliate by hanging the treason prisoners.

Gov. Robinson was taken by a mob at Lexington, Mo., while descending the Missouri in company with his wife. He was detained there for a few days; thence taken by way of Westport, to Franklin, within four miles of Lawrence; thence back to Kansas City, and up the Missouri, to Leavenworth, where he arrived on the eve of these murders on the Pottawatomie. The news of the massacre caused the most intense excitement. It was all that active pro-slavery men, who were warm personal friends of the Governor, some of whom were under lasting obligations to him for favors rendered in California, and on his way thither, to save him from violent death. Indeed, the people were wrought up to such a furious phrenzy that death was expected at any moment. An eye-witness of the scene told me that the cooler and better class of the citizens, thinking they were powerless to save him, wept like children as one by one they took him by the hand and bade him farewell.

The Congressional Investigating Committee were in session at Leavenworth. They could not proceed with business because of the excitement, hence removed to Kansas City, where they also found it impossible, with personal safety, to continue their investigations, and left for Washington, one of the members remaining long enough to obtain affidavits detailing the incidents of this awful tragedy, portions of which I have copied. In his minority report to Congress, he said of these murders:— 'In savage barbarity and demoniac cruelty they [have] scarcely an equal in the history of civilized man.'" The majority of the Committee were compelled to stultify themselves, and throw out important evidence they had already taken, in order to suppress the loathing details of the butchery.

A lady resident of Leavenworth, at the time the news of the tragedy reached that city, told me, on her way up the Missouri in the following spring, returning for the first time after the occurrence to Kansas, of its effects on the Free State population there. She said a public meeting of pro-slavery men was immediately called, when the account of the Pottawotomie massacre was narrated to the already-crazed pro-slavery mob. The most violent, denunciatory and threatening speeches were made. Resolutions were passed of a fiery character, setting forth that the first blood had been shed by the Free State men; that the midnight assassins were not satisfied with simply murdering their victims, but that they had mutilated them in a shameful manner. They declared that it was impossible for the abolitionists and the pro-slavery settlers to live together in Kansas and that the former must leave. She said a body of armed men marched through the streets, visiting each dwelling, and ordered every Free State man, woman and child to go at once to the Levee. They would not allow her to even close her house; but with her children she was marched to the river where she found hundreds of others. All were forced upon a steamer lying at the levee, including her husband who she found there. The Captain was ordered to take these involuntary passengers to Alton and there leave them. She remained in that city until the spring of 1857, when she returned with her husband and again settled in the Territory.

Mr. Phillips, in his "Conquest of Kansas," (a very singular title for a book whose author was supposed to be in favor of free institutions for that Territory,) speaking of this event, page 318, says:

"Citizens of Leavenworth who were known to be Free State men, were notified that they must leave the Territory. * * On the morning of the 28th of May, [four days after the murders, as the reader will observe,] the office of the Leavenworth *Herald* issued a reprint of a violent 'war' extra of the Westport paper, the design of which was to excite the border men to acts of violence against the Free State settlers of Kansas. In the forenoon of that day a pro-slavery meeting was held, at which Stringfellow and Gen. Richardson were prominent actors. At this meeting it was decreed that all persons who had taken an active part as Free State men must leave the Territory."

Mr. Phillips seems to ascribe these outrages, by the pro-slavery party at Leavenworth, to the appearance of the Investigating Committee; but the facts are, they were because the news of the murders on the Pottawotomie only reached them at that moment, by way of Westport and Kansas City, hence the reason of republishing the "war extra" from Westport.

Gov. Robinson was hurried away from Leavenworth, in the midst of this excitement, by the cooler headed pro-slavery men, across the prairies to Lecompton, where he joined the other prisoners under indictment for high treason on the 1st of June. It was owing to this event he was saved from violence.

But these excesses were not limited to Leavenworth. Steamers coming up the Missouri, loaded with Eastern passengers, were sent back to St. Louis; and all emigration by way of this great thoroughfare was suspended until autumn, and the arrival of Gov. Geary in the Territory. A reign of terror paralyzed every industry, and mob violence reigned supreme.

South of the river the times were no less exciting. The pro-slavery population on the Pottawotomie arose in mass, burned the cabins of Captain Brown's sons, (not his, for he never had any cabin in Kansas to burn,) drove off their stock, and it is probable their language to the daughter and daughter-in-law, who alone were in possession, was really insulting, for it is said to be true they represented the father and husband of these ladies, (very amiable people, by the way,) with having caused the murder of their friends, the Doyles, &c.

Henry Clay Pate, with his "Westport Sharpshooters," who were mounted, had escorted Gaius Jenkins and the writer from Westport to a point near Lecompton, where we arrived on the evening of the 19th of May. He was present, taking part with his command, at the sacking of Lawrence, on the 21st. Thence he visited Lecompton, where he learned, on the evening of the 25th, of the murders on the Pottawotomie. As every Missourian imagined himself a United States Marshal—many had commissions as deputy, and among this number was Pate himself—he resolved to arrest John Brown and his party, then augmented to nine. Without following his steps in detail to Palmyra and Prairie City, and noting the outrages which Pate perpetrated at these places, and in their vicinity, enough to ever cover his name with infamy, they came in contact, on the 2d of June, 1856, with old John, at a place on the Sante Fe road known as Black Jack. Whether any portion of Brown's force was with him at the massacre, the writer has no means of knowing. A collision came on. Capt. Shore, who had been watching Capt. Pate's movements after leaving Prairie City, with some 60 men, put in an appearance at a very opportune moment for the safety of the "Liberator; a very animated skirmish followed; Pate and his command were captured. Here occurred the famous "battle of Black Jack," in which Brown is represented as an invincible hero; instead of being arrested for murder, with the aid of the very large force of Capt. Shore, aided by Capt. Mewhinny, the pro-slavery marauders were captured. Pate was soon after re-released by United States troops, under Col. Sumner, and, with a severe reprimand, was ordered home to Missouri.

On the 6th of June, still in pursuit of the Pottawotomie murderers, was "fought" what is known in Kansas history, as the first battle of Osawotomie; but the fight consisted in a retreat of the pursued to the timber,—"skedaddling," we used to call it on the border,—while the pursuers ransacked and pillaged the town; and yet old John Brown is lauded by his biographers as the hero of this occasion, as he was at Black Jack, though he sought safety in the covert of the wood, as the others did. This statement I had confirmed while writing these pages, by a gentleman from Kansas, visiting friends in Rockford, who was in the *bush* with the other Free State men, and who, in answer to my direct inquiry, said there was not a gun fired in defense on that day. And thus heroes are made, on small occasions. And thus great battles are fought—on paper.

The so-called "second battle of Osawotomie" occurred on the 29th of August, 1856. It was precipitated on the town by an attack, by residents and others, driving off a party of Buford's men, who were encamped near, and who, like their associates all over the Territory, were guilty of every variety of wickedness. These men deserved severe punishment wherever found, during their stay in Kansas. Their expulsion, however, aroused the war spirit again; again inflammatory appeals were made to Missourians; another invasion was planned, and on the 29th of August, 1856, under the command of Gen. John W. Reed, of Independence, Mo., with some four hundred followers, Osawotomie was attacked. The citizens under various commands, in companies of ten to fifteen from the thick undergrowth surrounding the town, fired upon the invaders, and they, thinking "prudence the better part of valor," made a speedy retreat. Probably this repulsed army, of 400, became the nucleus of the 2,700 which marched on Lawrence on the 14th of September. The general understanding in Kansas was that Old John exhibited good fighting qualities at Osawotomie. He was engaged in a good cause, but whether he deserved more applause than Capt. Cline, Dr. Updegraff, or any other brave man there, the writer has no knowledge.

How many cases of violence, consisting of murders, arsons, robberies, rapes, &c., were perpetrated during that summer, which had their origin in excited passions, influenced by these transactions on the Pottawotomie, no human historian will ever know. It was the pro-slavery purpose to drive out the Free State settlers. They sought every pretext in their reach to justify their aggressions. The great misfortune was that too many of these were offered, and that the innocent had to suffer for the violence of his guilty neighbor.

NOT LIMITED TO KANSAS.

The effect of this massacre on the prosperity of Kansas was not limited to that Territory. A national party, with powerful anti-slavery proclivities, had recently sprung into being. It undertook the task of defending and sustaining the struggling Free State men, who had thrown themselves into the mighty chasm, made by the repeal of the Missouri Compromise of 1820. These Free State men, had resolved that the principles involved in that settlement of a vexed question, by their fathers, should still be maintained; that the broad and beautiful prairies of Kansas should never be cursed by the tread of the slave. They had gone from the comforts of their Eastern homes; had sacrificed business long established; had broken loose from all social and religious organizations, and abandoned parties to which they were dearly attached, and formed a new one, with the single motto of "Kansas a Free State." Now a new party was organized in the States, out of remnants of old ones, with the principle written in its platform, and emblazoned on its flag, and borne aloft by its standard bearer, "No more Slave States, No More Slave Territory; Freedom to the Republic, JUSTICE TO KANSAS!"

But on the very eve of the first organization of that party, while every pulsation of the genuinely good was beating in full sympathy with "bleeding Kansas," and they were solemnly determined to right our wrongs, and correct the abuses of false legislation, they were met with these excesses by the men they would serve!

The horrible details of that midnight butchery on the Pottawotomie, were dwelt upon, and passed from mouth to mouth; the opposition press, both North and South, took up the damning tale and passed it on. Whole columns of leaders from week to week, with startling headlines, liberally-distributed capitals, and frightful exclamation points, filled all the newspapers; while each public speaker, who wished to inflame the already excited populace, in glowing rhetoric, would depict the ghastly spectacle of five men torn from their beds at midnight, and ruthlessly slaughtered by savage, ferocious and unfeeling Free State men.

The Republicans denied the allegations; they set up an *alibi*; they charged the butchery and mutilation on the Camanches; they said the killing was done in self-defense; they apologized for it in various ways; when forced to the wall they attempted justification; but, meet it as they would, there was the appalling outrage; the deep, dark and damning bloodspots which would not disappear at their bidding.

When the autumn elections came on, so successful had the opposition been in ringing these charges on the country, the friends of Kansas were overborne by superior numbers, and another four years of misrule by the Democratic party, under its corrupt leaders, was inaugurated. The oppressed in Kansas saw another term of struggle and violence before them.

As an actor in those exciting times, watching the progress of the political canvass from my prairie prison, surrounded continually by the gleam of the sabre, the musket and bayonet of Federal troops, with a large list of exchanges for the *Herald of Freedom*, daily received in camp, and little to do but read them, I do soberly aver and believe, twenty four years thereafter, that had it not been for the massacre of the three Doyles, of Wilkinson and Sherman, by self-styled Free State men on the Pottawotomie, the Republican party would have been successful in that memorable campaign of 1856, and our period of enslavement would have been four years abridged. But perhaps we should take cheer from classic story, and "Weep not for the lost leaves of Cybele."

As the horrors of the Spanish Inquisition; the bloody butcheries, martyrdoms, crimes and excesses of the middle ages, with the massacre of St. Bartholomew at a later period, paved the way, and added new impetus to the Reformation, which gave rise to subsequent liberal thought, with full toleration of all forms of religious and non-religious faith, and a larger comprehension of man's final destiny; so the outcome of this awful tragedy traced by the pen of the casuist, shows the defeat of Republicanism in 1856; the prolongation of our Kansas ills; the rebellion; a nation rolled in blood; the conflagration of cities; the complete upheaval of society; crimes unparalleled in the world's history; general bankruptcy; and every heart filled with deepest woe. In bold and cheering contrast we have the disenthralment of a race; the greater freedom of the masses; education more widely diffused; larger religious liberty, and a more glorious future than was ever before witnessed by aspiring humanity, or predicted by inspired prophet.

As well, however, to give credit to Torquemada, the father of the Inquisition, for our present religious freedom, as to old John Brown, and the massacre on the Pottawotomie, for the freedom of Kansas, or our present and prospective prosperity.

THE SUMMER OF 1856.

How Capt. Brown spent the summer of 1856, other than avoiding an arrest, and with his "twelve or fifteen new recruits," as he calls his *army*, defending Osawotomie, we have but little knowledge. He represents that in that "bloody battle" there were, of the invaders, "thirty-one or two killed, and from forty to fifty wounded." This assertion was as positively denied by the attacking party. It is certain there were three killed on the Free State side, to wit: Fred Brown, Mr. Partridge and Mr. Williams.

Sometime during the summer of 1856, a Santa Fe train was captured by Free State men. These trains consisted, usually, of twenty to sixty very large wagons, carrying some two or more tons of freight, consisting of general merchandise, drawn by six mules. The wagons were covered with white canvas, and when moving over the prairies, stretched out over a long distance. The sight was truly imposing. Minus the speed they would remind the observer of the immense freight trains of the Atchison and Santa Fe Railroad moving in the same direction to-day.

These mule trains were fitted out in Westport, Mo., and Kansas City, and through them was carried on the almost limitless commerce between the States and New Mexico.

Who was concerned in the capture of this train mentioned I never knew, as I was a prisoner at the time, and our field of observation was not large. The Free State newspapers of the Territory were all suspended, and it is even questionable if mention would have been made of it, for *prudential reasons*, had all been in successful operation; for we were extremely careful, in those exciting times, not to expose the dereliction or excesses of our own party friends. If I don't forget it, and a good place occurs, I will tell "A Case in Point," at a considerable later date, in illustration.

The magnitude, however, of the capture

of an entire Santa Fe train made a little riffle of excitement at the time, and the responsibility with the public seemed divided between Dr. Ephraim Cutter, E. B. Whitman and old John Brown. Whether any or all of these personages were concerned in the capture, I do not know; but I have an indefinite recollection that there was a wordy quarrel, or misunderstanding at least, between the parties implicated, in regard to the division of plunder. My only reason for thinking John Brown was not concerned in it, is that I find no mention of it in "Redpath's Life of the Captain," whereas had the "Liberator" been even the humblest private in the affair, he would have been magnified into a leader; the details of the capture would have extended through several chapters, describing each incident of the battle, the various strategical movements employed to surround the "greasers," the deafening roar of musketry, the clash of crossed sabres, the wild shrieks of the captors, the dying groans of the defeated teamsters, closing with a poem in Homeric verse, from that brilliant poet Raelf, preserving in song for future ages a glowing account of the gallant affair. He could not have done less than quoted the last stanza from "Brown's Address to His Men;" page 156, of his "Life of Brown:"

We must conquer, we must slaughter,
We are God's rod, and His ire
Will their blood shall flow like water
In Jehovah's dread name—Fire!

This will give the reader an idea of what the brilliant historian *could* have done with a very trifling capital. As Redpath was not in the Territory at the time, and the Byronic poet did not arrive until, I think the 10th of October following, this may account for the loss of this glowing description of the event.

JOHN BROWN'S BIOGRAPHER.

I have had frequent occasion to refer to, or quote from "Redpath's Life of John Brown," and shall have still further use for him, as we advance with these "Reminiscences." The reader must of course desire to know the character of the author, and the stand-point from which he wrote. I take pleasure in furnishing this information, by stating that Redpath claimed great intimacy with Brown in Kansas; was an indorser of the invasion at Harper's Ferry; wrote largely in its interest; was selected by the John Brown family to write a "Life" of their head; into whose hands, the letters, writings and sketches of the Captain were placed; and who agreed to divide the profits accruing from the sale of the book with the family. Under the head of Professional Letter Writers, I shall have occasion to mention Mr. Redpath again.

In 1859, Redpath published a book of 365 pages, entitled "The Roving Editor." It came from the press sometime before the Harper's Ferry raid of Old John. From some pages it is very evident the book was prepared with special purpose to encourage and incite a servile insurrection.

I copy from page 306 of that revolutionary book:—

"But is insurrection possible?"

"I believe that it is. The only thing that has hitherto prevented a universal revolt, is the impossibility of forming extended combinations. This the slave code effectually prevents. To attain this end, therefore, the agency of white men is needed."

"Are there men ready for this holy work?"

"I thank God that there are. There are men who are tired of praising the French patriots—who are ready to *be* Lafayettes and Kosciuskos to the slaves."

"Do you ask for a programme of action?"

"The negroes and Southrons have taught us. The slaves of the Dismal Swamp, the maroons of Florida, the

Free-State men of Kansas, have pointed out the method. The South committed suicide when it compelled the free squatters to resort to guerilla warfare, *and to study it both as a mode of subsistence and a science.* For the mountains, the swamps and morasses of the South, are peculiarly adapted to this mode of combat, and there are a number of young men trained to the art in the Kansas ravines, who are eager for an opportunity of avenging their slain comrades, on the real authors of their death, in the forests and plantations of the Carolinas and Georgia."

"*Will you aid them—will you sustain them? Are you in favor of a servile insurrection?*"

"Tell God in acts."

This book from which I cite is dedicated by Redpath "To Captain John Brown, of Kansas." On the fourth page of the Dedication, at its close, he says:—

"You went to Kansas when the trouble broke out there—not to 'settle' or 'speculate'—or from idle curiosity; but for one stern, solitary purpose—*to have a shot at the South. So did I.*

"To you, therefore, my senior in years as in service to the slave, I dedicate this work."

Under the sub-head of "My Object," page 300, Redpath informs us why he traveled through the South before going to Kansas, in 1855, and says it was to "disseminate discontentment" among the slaves on certain conditions, which he names. He then adds:

"I believed that a civil war between the North and South would ultimate in insurrection, and that the Kansas troubles would probably create a military conflict of the sections. Hence I left the South, and went to Kansas; *and endeavored, personally and by my pen, to precipitate a revolution.* That we failed—for I was not alone in this desire—was owing to the influence of prominent Republican statesmen, whose unfortunately conservative character of counsel—which it was impossible to openly resist—effectually baffled all our hopes: hopes which Democratic action was auspiciously promoting."

The insurrection was finally set on foot in the South, agreeably to Redpath's plans. He was a valiant warrior on paper; the inciter, aider and abettor of a servile and warlike revolution, as shown by the foregoing extracts; yet he was not there to lead, or assist, or in any manner to endanger his own person, but realized the oft-quoted couplet of Hudibras, that

"He who fights and runs away,
May live to fight another day."

I am glad to do justice to Redpath, and say that after the execution of his patron saint; after he discovered that the public did not sanction his wild schemes of murder and violence; and after he had written the "Life of John Brown," he engaged in the Hayti emigration movement, and published in Boston, a paper entitled *The Pine and Palm.* The following extracts from that paper I made at the time of its publiation, but neglected to note its date. It is in words following:

"A PREPARATORY WORD.—Having become sincerely convinced that many of the political doctrines that I have advocated in my writings are dangerous and abhorrent to the higher insight—the murderous policy, for example, of inciting the slaves to insurrection which I have urged repeatedly, and with terrible mistaken zeal—I wish to announce here that I shall retire from any participation in the political management of this journal, excepting for the purpose of retracting past errors, until such time as I feel that I have attained a clearer and more humane and Christian view of the duties of the freeman to the enslaved.

"I shall confine myself exclusively to the editing of the outside pages of the paper. The name of the acting editors will be duly announced.—The articles signed with an (*) were mine; of these I will retract many; my associates, who indicate their respective writings by the initial L., and by the marks †, ‡, §, are alone responsible for their thoughts thus labeled. I repudiate my war doctrines, utterly and forever.

"JAMES REDPATH."

In a later number of *The Pine and Palm,* I find a longer statement, in which

Redpath gives the reason for the sudden change in his views. I quote briefly:

"It is right now that I should confess, publicly and contritely, that my recent change in political policy proceeds solely and irresistibly from a change of heart—from an acceptance, fully and unreserved, of the doctrines and plan of salvation of our Lord and Savior Jesus Christ. * * Not the blood of the slaveholder, but the blood of the Redeemer, can truly free the slave. * * Hitherto I have conducted this movement (Haytien emigration,) from a sense of duty to man; henceforth I shall seek to conduct it as a duty to God and *man*. May his Holy Spirit guide, direct, and uphold me!
JAMES REDPATH."

In another clipping, which I made about the same time, a like confession was made in regard to another very bad habit he had fallen into touching his veracity. This vice had grown upon him until it seemed a part of his being. In the burning of the *Herald of Freedom* building and contents, at the Quantrell Raid on Lawrence, in 1863, all the files of my papers were wholly consumed, with bound volumes of many other Kansas journals which I had carefully preserved. There were also a large and choice collection of excerpts saved for future use, among which probably was the one referred to, and it was lost. I greatly regret this, for then I could have done this famous letter writer, biographer and author further valuable service. That he was sincerely "contrite" for this evil habit, *at the time he wrote*, there is no doubt. I hope his reformation was permanent.

JOHN BROWN, JR.

John Brown, Jr., and H. H. William were brought into the camp, near Lecompton, about the 15th of June, 1856 and were held as prisoners with us. They were indicted on the 27th of May, at Paola, then Lykins county, charged with "conspiracy to resist the collection of taxes." John was also suspicioned with responsibility for the Pottawotomie murders, but I am glad to say there was no truth whatever in this allegation. He became an occupant of my tent, and remained with me some time after he was brought into camp. He was partly insane; his mind seemed continually running on the Pottawotomie massacre, and he appeared to suppose he was under arrest for that offence. During the entire period he was with us—nearly three months—whenever that event was mentioned in his hearing his eyes would flash and sparkle like a madman's. He would exhibit the wildest excitement, and express himself, in the severest terms at the enormity of the outrage. On several occasions I attempted to ally his irritation by offering an apology for it. He replied invariably: "There can be no apology for such a transaction. Every feature of it was too barbarous to admit of an apology." And then I would divert his mind as speedily as possible, engage his thoughts on some other subject, when he would gradually regain his composure.

In his ravings about these murders on the Pottawotomie, John, Jr., told me of the incidents lying between his disbanding his command, when the news of the massacre reached him, on the morning after its committal, until his arrest. He said his best friends in Osawotomie turned the "cold shoulder" on him, when he arrived in the town ; a public meeting of Free State men was soon held, which repudiated it, and denounced the actors; he called on his wife and child, and made his way to the bottom lands, where he secreted himself behind logs and trees. He forded the river several times to avoid exposure. A severe storm of rain and lightning came on, and he thought, in the flashes, he could see his pursuers. He said he suffered for food; but his wife occasionally found and relieved him. Finally, at the suggestion of his friends, he voluntarily surrendered himself to the civil authorities, and was taken in charge by federal troops. He was removed to Paola; thence to Tecumseh, where he had a hearing before U. S. Commissioner Hoagland, and was sent to camp for safe keeping. He represented that he was bound with ropes and chains, and was compelled to "trot along," thus bound, between two horsemen, for forty miles, in a hot June sun. How much of these statements were real, and how much imaginary, it would be difficult to determine. His friends, outside of Kansas, say he was made insane by the cruel treatment he received as a prisoner, and John himself is still laboring under that delusion; but I think his insanity was induced by the severe fatigue incident to his long and exciting march towards Lawrence; the nervous shock he received when informed of the sacking of that town, and his wearisome return journey; the news of the massacre falling so unexpectedly on an extremely sensitive nature, followed by being suspicioned by his friends as an accomplice; and his exposure, loss of sleep and anxiety of mind while hiding from his pursuers. I am sustained in these opinions by the letter of old John Brown, directed to Mr. Sanborn, already quoted, under the head of "Newly Discovered Evidence." Speaking of his being accused of the murders, Brown continues:

"John's company soon afterwards disbanded, and also the Osawotomie men. John tried to hide for several days, but from the feelings of the ungrateful conduct of those who ought to have stood by him, excessive fatigue, anxiety and loss of sleep, became quite *insane*, and in that condition gave up, or, as we are told, was betrayed at Osawotomie into the hands of the Bogus men."

John told me during his confinement, of a plan, on the part of his father, to carry the war into Missouri. He showed that in his estimation the scheme was a practical one to make slave property valueless on the other side of the Territorial line. He reasoned that a constant agitation, by running off the negroes, would make slave property so insecure that the large holders would be compelled to either emancipate their "chattles," or sell them South. In either contingency it would ultimate in the abolition of slavery in that State. In fact the whole plan of a servile insurrection was developed in these conversations, his father being the leader, identical in every essential particular with that which, three years later, was attempted in Virginia, the difference—Missouri was the point of attack instead of Virginia; and the prairies of Kansas were the base of operations instead of the mountains of the Old Dominion.

John's wife and young son came into camp a short time after his arrival, and remained until the discharge of the treason prisoners, on the 10th of September, on our personal recognizances. John, Jr., and Mr. Williams were left in custody. The difficulty of their detention being mentioned to the Court by the military officer in command, they were allowed to depart on giving bail in the sum of $5,000 each. I acknowledged myself bound in that sum for John's appearance. I may say in this connection the bond was forfeited; but I was never prosecuted under it. By a late letter of Mr. Brown's, I observe that he is under the impression that he was indicted for high treason, but this is a mistake.

On breaking up camp Mr. Brown and wife accompanied me to my home at Lawrence, where he remained for a few days until after the 14th of September invasion, and the excitement following it had passed, when, with his wife, father, and brothers, he started for the States, going north to Nebraska, and overland through Iowa.

GOV. GEARY.

Before release from imprisonment, on the 10th of September, I received a very interesting letter from Hon. Morrow B. Lowry, of Erie, Pa., whom I had known from boyhood, accompanied with a letter of introduction to Gov. Geary. Mr. Lowry had always acted with the Democratic party, until the nomination of John C. Fremont, when, resolved to aid in righting the wrongs done to Kansas, he gave his earnest support to the Republican leader. Mr. Lowry requested me to present the letter of introduction to our new Governor, as soon as possible after his arrival in the Territory. He wrote that he knew Col. Geary intimately; had served one term with him in the Pennsylvania Legislature; that he was a gentleman in the full sense of that term, and that the Free State men could rely upon his integrity and honor. He desired me to give him my confidence and receive his. He stated he had written Gov. Geary in a similar spirit in regard to myself.

Gov. Geary arrived at Leavenworth on the 9th of September, on the 10th reached Lecompton, and on Friday, the 12th, visited Lawrence. I met him at the Cincinnati House; presented him Mr. Lowry's letter, and had a brief interview. The Governor mentioned that he received, on the eve of leaving his home for Kansas, a letter from his friend Lowry in regard to me, and that he would take great pleasure in favoring me in any way in his power.

The Governor had already distributed large numbers of his proclamations, ordering all bodies of armed men to lay down their arms and retire to their homes and ordinary occupations. He declared his intention to protect the Territory from further violence. I walked with him to various influential citizens, whom I introduced. In answer to questions I frequently heard propounded, "Governor, do you think it is safe for us to go to our homes," he invariably replied: "You had better stay in town a few days longer, for mutual protection; but be careful that you do nothing in violation of the spirit of my proclamation. To defend yourselves against an attack, will not incur my displeasure."

On that afternoon, or the following morning, Gov. Geary, with his escort, returned to Lecompton.

A CRISIS APPROACHING.

At the time Gov. Geary's arrival in the Territory, Lawrence was a military camp. Woodson, the pro-slavery Secretary, under Gov. Shannon, was the acting Governor, and was running things with a high hand. All the roads leading to Lawrence were blockaded by armed bodies of Southern marauders, and every day violence was perpetrated upon Free State citizens. Guerilla parties of Free State men were also roving the Territory, committing depredations on pro-slavery men. Between these bodies there was no safety for any one.

Gov. Geary, in his "Farewell Address to the People of Kansas," dated March 12, 1857, manuscript copy of which was mailed me from St. Louis, and published in the *Herald of Freedom* of April 18th, '57, thus graphically and truthfully describes the condition of the Territory, on his first arrival—the time of which I am writing. He says:

"I reached Kansas, and entered upon the discharge of my official duties in the most gloomy hour of her history. Desolation and ruin reigned on every hand; homes and firesides were deserted; the smoke of burning dwellings darkened the atmosphere; women and children, driven from their habitations, wandered over the prairies and among the woodlands, or sought refuge and protection even among the Indian tribes. The highways were infested with numerous predatory bands, and the towns were fortified and garrisoned by armies of conflicting partizans, each excited almost to frenzy, and determined upon mutual extermination. Such was, without exaggeration, the condition of the Territory at the period of my arrival."

In Lawrence, where the people had resorted from the country for security, the masses were subsisting on just what foraging parties could pick up through the country, even bringing in unthreshed wheat and oats, treading out the grain, and grinding in coffee mills. Teams sent to Kansas City or Leavenworth for supplies were sure to be confiscated by the Border Ruffians, and the teamsters were robbed and outraged in some form. I think there were full 800 Free State men in town on the Governor's arrival; and yet, when with tears in their eyes I heard parties tell the Governor the necessitous condition in which they had left their families, and how anxious they were to go to their relief, the Governor would reply: "You had better remain in Lawrence a few days longer, but only for defence."

I will not at *this time* detail all the facts *I know* in regard to this subject, as they will be more properly treated of in my "Reminiscences of Gen. Lane," which I am invited to write. *I will say that history needs correction, badly, at this point.* Suffice it for the present, the entire defences of Lawrence were removed, leaving not to exceed two hundred men in town, and (save the "Stubbs," who were armed with Sharp's rifles, and who I wish to say were always on hand and faithful to every trust,) scarcely any organized force whatever.

ANOTHER INVASION.

Beginning at about 2 o'clock, of Sunday afternoon, the 14th of September, 1856, every little while a messenger would arrive in Lawrence, on a foaming steed, from the direction of Missouri, and in hurried words state that a large body of armed men were rapidly marching on the town. The numbers of the enemy were variously estimated at from 1,500 to 2,000. The earnestness in which the news was imparted, the appearance of the horses, and frequent repetition of reports were sufficient assurances of danger. Several expresses were quickly dispatched, by different routes, to Gov. Geary, at Lecompton, one of which I forwarded with a note, and Gov. Robinson did the same with another. Other parties were equally active.

Four days before, the treason prisoners had been discharged, leaving Col. Patrick St. George Cooke, who had them in custody, with a battery and full regiment of United States cavalry stationed within two miles of Lecompton. Our hopes of succor in this trying moment was in the interposition of these troops between us and the invading forces.

The *Herald of Freedom* building was a high three-story structure, with stairs reaching the roof, which was flat. From this point I watched in the direction from which we expected the enemy, occasionally descending to mingle with the citizens to see what arrangements were being made for defense. The ladies in my residence, which was divided from the office by a narrow alley only, were making cartridges, while others were bringing bullets and powder from neighboring places. I was a deeply interested party, for teams were then on the road for my new press, type and fixtures, and I was soon expecting their arrival.

About 5 o'clock a large party of horsemen, estimated at 400, were seen approaching from towards Franklin. They were within, probably, two miles of the town. The fact was announced, when, descending from my point of observation, taking two or three loaded guns, accompanied by my sister, Mrs. Mary A. Mandell, and my sister in-law, Miss A. W. Gleason, they bearing cartridges, we made our way to entrenchments thrown up in the autumn previous, I think, near Vermont and Henry streets. We entered one of these and watched all that transpired, ready to sell our lives as dearly as possible in defence of our homes and each other. I remember seeing old John Brown pass near, going towards some other entrenchment; but I heard no speech, no directions, no counsels, no command of any character. He wore no ensignia of rank, and carried neither sword or gun. Col. J. B. Abbott was understood to be in command. Yet, as the forces were unorganized, and the feeling was universal that a vigorous and successful defence was the condition on which we should escape; we needed no commander in such an emergency. The threats that reached us were that we were "to be wiped out." We numbered not to exceed two hundred, while the advancing enemy was believed to equal four hundred, and back of these was a large army, how many we did not know.

As the invaders neared the town the Stubbs, consisting of some sixty young men, armed with Sharp's rifles, advanced to meet them. A braver or truer body of men never set foot on Kansas soil. They were justly the pride of the town. There was not a man among them who would not have deemed it a pleasure to die in preference to turning his face from the foe. Many of these men afterwards fell under command of Col. Deitzler, at Wilson's creek, where Gen. Lyon was killed. Their names adorn the brightest pages of Kansas history.

The Stubbs fired a few shots at the approaching enemy, and one of the invaders fell from his horse, which galloped away riderless. At this occurrence they retraced their steps to Franklin and rejoined the main army. They proved to be an advanced mounted guard, which had gone out to "feel" of the Free State men, and see if they were disposed to offer any resistance to their entering the town.

The general invading force had been collected from various points in Missouri, and had rendezvoused at Westport, under Gen. Heiskell, responsive to a proclamation from Acting-Governor Woodson. They learned from spies, who were at Lawrence, on the arrival of Gov. Geary, and who remained until Col. Harvey, in obedience to an order from Gen. Lane, had crossed the river and gone to Hickory Point, *in defiance of the Governor's proclamation*, taking with him the almost entire defenses of the town. Dispatches, it seems, were sent to Westport, and on the 12th, the enemy set out determined to reach Lawrence in this unprotected condition, and destroy it before Gov. Geary could interpose any obstruction. They had purposed to reach their point of destination on the afternoon of Sunday, and complete their bloody work. Instead, the forty miles of travel for a large body of badly organized soldiery, which proved to consist of 2,700 men, unaccustomed to long marches delayed them, and on reaching Franklin the infantry and four pieces of cannon were halted, while the cavalry advanced; seeing a fight was inevitable, returned and delayed their intended assault upon the town until the following morning.

Reader, be patient. I am trying at this point to correct much false history, and have entered into greater detail than I would under other circumstances.

FEDERAL INTERPOSITION.

About 9 o'clook Sunday night the heavy rumbling of wagons, and the rapid clatter of horses' hoofs, descending th elevated plat eau from the old California road to Lawrence, gave assurance that protection had reached us in the form of the United States cavalry, a battery of six cannon, and a thousand well-armed and thoroughly drilled soldiers, under the command of that brave old warrior, Col. Cooke, who, two years after, when tendered the command of the rebel troops of Virginia, by the Governor of his native State, in substance replied, that

"Though I love my mother, on whose bosom I was nursed, yet I owe allegiance to my father more, who reared me, gave me my military education, trusted me with a commission in his army, under whose flag I have spent the best years of my life, and, though sorry to raise an arm against her who gave me birth, am resolved, if need be, to die in that father's defence."

I had made Col. Cooke's acquaintance while a prisoner, indeed had commenced writing a series of personal sketches of him, for publication, which he himself kindly furnished me, but which were cut short, long before their completion, by our unexpected discharge. His opportune arrival before Lawrence, relieved further anxiety, and, like hundreds of other weary ones, I retired for the night, after seeing the troops entering camp between the invaders at Franklin and our own greatly loved pioneer city of Kansas.

GOV. GEARY'S STATEMENT.

To conclude this narration, Gov. Geary told me, soon after the events I have recorded transpired, that on his way up the Missouri he saw these invaders organizing, and learned they were marshaling their forces at Westport, Mo; that he hurried forward as rapidly as possible, prepared his proclamation to head them off, and resolved that no injury should come to Lawrence in any contingency; that this was the reason he suggested to persons inquiring of him "that it would be better to remain in Lawrence a few days longer," and that the invaders had stolen a march on him, and set themselves down before the town several days earlier than he expected.

The Governor said, on receipt of the first note, which reached him, quite late in the afternoon of Sunday, he immediately wrote and dispatched to camp, two miles distant, the following:

EXECUTIVE OFFICE, Lecompton, Kan.T.
Sept. 14, 1856.

COL. P. St. GEORGE COOKE:—Remove your entire command, with all possible dispatch, to Lawrence, for the defence of that town. I will accompany you in person. JOHN W. GEARY, Governor.

Early in the morning of the 15th, Gov. Geary issued the following order:

EXECUTIVE OFFICE, Kansas T.,
In Camp near Lawrence,
Sept. 15, 1856.

COL. P. St. GEORGE COOKE: Interpose your command before Lawrence, and allow no armed body to enter that town. Call the people of that city to your aid, if you need assistance. Disregard any order coming from me to the contrary, unless given in person.

JOHN W. GEARY, Governor Kan. T.

Gov. Geary, with a small escort, accompanied by Col. Cooke, rode to Franklin and had an interview with the commanding officers, and the head conspirator, Dave Atchison. They claimed to be there in accordance with a proclamation issued by Acting Gov. Woodson; that they appeared in the capacity of Kansas militia, though they would not deny the fact that they came from Missouri; that they had an enrolled force of 2,400, and about 300 stragglers who were not formally organized, but would do effective work if an engagement took place.

The Governor caused his proclamation to be read to the entire force; assured the invaders that he had a federal force sufficient to maintain the peace of the Territory, and that their services would not be required in that direction.

After the Governor retired the leaders held a long consultation, and, finally, reluctantly consented to retrace their steps to Missouri. A portion of them made the circuitous route by way of Lecompton, and committed gross outrages *en route*, among others stealing several horses, and murdering a gentleman by the name of Buffum. Gov. Geary attempted to bring the villains to justice, but was thwarted through the interposition of a corrupt judiciary.

THE PRO-SLAVERY ACCOUNT.

I compile from an anonymous writer in the St. Louis *Evening News* of September 24th, the following version of this affair from a "Border Ruffian" standpoint. I use the language of the writer, only slightly abridged:—

"The Missourians, true to their word, marched from Westport, on the 13th, to attack Lawrence. The army was composed of one regiment of foot and two of mounted men—in all ",400 men, attended by four pieces of artillery. Gen. Heiskell was in command. On the 13th and 14th, the army marched forty miles, reaching Franklin, four miles from Lawrence. The advance guard, when about three miles from Franklin, was fired on by the picket guard of the Lawrence army, and one man was killed. The main body was hurried up as rapidly as possible, for the purpose of attacking Lawrence that evening. By the time it reached Franklin it was night, and the contemplated attack was postponed. The army encamped at Franklin, intending to make the assault next day, the 15th.

"At midnight an express arrived with information that Col. Cooke had been sent by Gov. Geary, who was urgently solicited by the people of Lawrence to interpose for their protection.

"On the 15th Gov. Geary arrived at Franklin and had a consultation with the officers of the invading army. He told them he was prepared to enforce the laws, to arrest offenders, crush out insurrection, and suppress disorder with the aid of the troops under his command; that the interposition of the troops under Gen. Heiskell was no longer necessary. In view of these facts he urged the Missourians to disband, and abandon their projected attack on Lawrence.

"Gen. Atchison, Gen. Reid and Col. Titus urged compliance with the Governor's proposal. The Governor withdrew from the conference.

"A meeting was immediately organized, with Gen. Atchison in the chair. Resolutions were passed declaring that relying on the protection promised to peaceable settlers by the Governor, they, the invading army, would disband and return to their homes."

REDPATH'S STATEMENT.

In his "Life of Old John Brown," Redpath devotes thirteen pages to the details of "Brown's Defence of Lawrence." To read it, with its gorgeous display of rhetoric, and brilliant scintillations of genius, not omitting, "not *fiction* but *poetry*," as Mrs. Robinson happily styles it, the reader would suppose that there, in Lawrence, on the afternoon of the 14th of September, 1856, and during the long night which followed, was fought one of the most destructive battles recorded in American history; and that to old John Brown's genius, and great military experience and gallantry, the people were indebted for their salvation, and the city saved from complete destruction. I quote from page 163, to its conclusion, omitting all the fine descriptions not necessary to a complete comprehension of the facts:

"The inquiry was next, 'Who shall be that leader?' * * It was no sooner known that Capt. Brown was in town, than he was unanimously voted general-in-chief for the day. The principal portion of the people had assembled in Main street, opposite the post office; [There is no Main street in Lawrence,] and Capt. Brown, standing upon a dry goods box in their midst, addressing them somewhat as follows: [Here follows a speech. Probably all who heard it were killed in the terrible fight(?) which followed.] * * Having thus taught them in the arts of war, he commenced his preparations for defence. * * Capt. Brown was always active and on the alert, visiting every part of the town, and all the

fortifications, in person, giving directions, and exhorting every man to keep cool, and do his duty, and his reward would be an approving conscience.   *   *   *
About five o'clock in the afternoon their advance guard, consisting of 400 horsemen, crossed the Wakarusa, and presented themselves in sight of town about two miles off, where they halted, and arranged themselves for battle, fearing perhaps to come within too close range of Sharp's rifle balls. Brown's movements now were a little on the offensive order, for he *ordered* out all the Sharpe's riflemen from every part of the town—in all not more than forty or fifty—marched them a half mile into the prairie, and arranged them three paces apart, in a line parallel with that of the enemy, and then they lay down upon their faces in the grass."

Let us leave them "lying on their faces," certainly a poor couch, skip over all the intermediate minute descriptions of incidents, the meeting of the beligerents "face to face," "half a mile apart and a cornfield between," the hurrying down of the sun in "anticipation of a fratricidal strife," the good deeds of the angel in "spreading her mantle over the earth," and the reflections of the author in regard to "the distant Aidenn," and, in modern parlance "pitch in" the thickest of the fight. Don Quixote's battle with the wind mills was nowhere. Listen:

"The distance now between the contending armies was such as to give Sharpe's rifle balls, that were fired with precision, a deadly effect; as was evinced by the fact that several horses were found riderless. In a few moments the firing became general, and in the darkness, and otherwise stillness of the night, the continual flash, flash, flash of these engines of death along the line of living fire, presented a scene the appearance of which was at once not only terrible but sublimely beautiful. From fear that the few men detailed to meet the enemy would be surrounded in the darkness, by the superior numbers of horsemen, and cut to pieces, a twelve-pound brass piece, under guard of twelve men, was sent to their assistance; but before it had arrived upon the ground, the foe had become panic-stricken and fled."

No wonder, for the brass piece mentioned did execution that day some twenty miles distant, in the vicinity of Hickory Point.

I will not disturb the slumbers of T., nor the historian of this bloody battle, nor the "General-in Chief," by entering the "breast work;" nor listen to the "Liberator's" recital of his trials as given on pages 167–8,, but give audience at once to Richard Realf, who, Redpath says, "died on his passage from England," where he had gone for funds to aid in the Harper's Ferry Raid, but which the newspapers said last year, had just suicided in San Francisco. "He who has tears to shed, prepare to shed them now!"

THE DEFENCE OF LAWRENCE.

All night, upon the guarded hill,
  Until the stars were low,
Wrapped round as with Jehovah's will,
  We waited for the foe;
All night the silent sentinels
  Moved by like gliding ghosts;
All night the fancied warning bells
  Held all men to their posts.

We heard the sleeping prairies breathe,
  The forest's human moans,
The hungry gnashing of the teeth
  Of wolves on bleaching bones;
We marked the roar of rushing fires,
  The neigh of frightened steeds,
And voices as of far-off lyres
  Among the river reeds.

We were but thirty-nine who lay
  Beside our rifles then;
We were but thirty-nine, and they
  Were twenty hundred men.
Our lean limbs shook and reeled about,
  Our feet were gashed and bare,
And all the breezes shredded out
  Our garments in the air.

Sick, sick, at all the woes which spring
  Where falls the Southron's rod,
Our very souls had learned to cling
  To Freedom as to God;
And so we never thought of fear,
  In all those stormy hours,
For every mother's son stood near
  The awful, unseen powers.

And twenty hundred men had met,
  And sworn an oath of hell
That, ere the morrow's sun might set,
  Our smoking homes should te'
A tale of ruin and of wrath,
  And damning hate in store,
To bar the freeman's western path
  Against him evermore.

They came: the blessed Sabbath day,
  That soothed our swollen veins,
Like God's sweet benediction, lay
  On all the singing plains;
The valleys shouted to the sun,
  The great woods clapped their hands,
And joy and glory seemed to run
  Like rivers through the lands.

They came: our daughters and our wives,
  And men whose heads were white,
Rose suddenly into kingly lives,
  And walked forth to the fight;
And we drew aim along our guns,
  And calmed our quickening breath;
Then, as is meet for Freedom's sons,
  Shook loving hands with Death.

And when three hundred of the foe
  Rode up in scorn and pride,
Whoso had watched us then might know
  That God was on our side;
For all at once, a mighty thrill
  Of grandeur through us swept,
And strong and swiftly down the hill
  Like Gideons we leapt.

And all throughout that Sabbath day
  A wall of fire we stood,
And held the battled foe at bay,
  And streaked the ground with blood;
And when the sun was very low,
  They wheeled their stricken ranks,
And passed on, wearily and slow,
  Beyond the river banks.

Beneath the everlasting stars,
  We bended child-like knees,
And thanked God for the shining scars
  Of his large victories;
And some, who lingered, said they heard
  Such wondrous music pass,
As though a seraph's voice had stirred
  The pulses of the grass.

CAPT. BROWN'S STATEMENT.

I have given the reader my own account of the defence of Lawrence, on the 14th of September, 1856, and minutely stated my means of information and observation. I have given the pro slavery account of the affair, as furnished by members of their own party, and published at the time in one of their own papers. I have copied from Redpath his account of the invasion, and showed what an exciting and prolonged battle was fought, in his *frenzied imagination*, on this occasion.

Old John Brown, when before the Massachusetts Legislature, in February, 1857, five months only after the event, made mention of it, which I copy from Redpath's life, page 181. He said:

"I know well that on or about the 14th of September, 1856, a large force of Missourians and other ruffians, said by Gov. Geary to be twenty-seven hundred in numbers, invaded the Territory, burned Franklin, and, while the smoke of that place was going up behind them, they, on the same day, made their appearance in full view of, and within about a mile of Lawrence; and I know of no reason why they did not attack that place, except that about one hundred Free State men *volunteered* to go out, and did go out on the open plain before the town, and give them the offer of a fight; which, after getting *scattering shots* from our men, they declined, and retreated back towards Franklin. I saw that whole thing."

The Chairman of the Committee, before whom the above statement was made, inquired "Who commanded the Free State men at Lawrence?" Redpath, page 183, gives the answer in these words:

"His answer was characteristic of the man, whose courage was only equalled by his modesty and worth. He explained how bravely our boys acted—gave every one the credit but himself. When again asked who commanded them, he said—*no one;* that he was asked to take the command, but *refused*, and only acted as their adviser."

Here we have the positive, unqualified, and *truthful* statement of old John Brown, that he did not command on that occasion. That he was requested by somebody to do so is very probable; but it could not have come from any authorized party without the writer's knowledge, for he was in a position of all men, to know what was transpiring on that day in Lawrence.

On three separate and distinct occasions old John Brown has been credited with being the "Defender of Lawrence." First, he appears in the city with his sons, in December, 1855, and is arrested for insubordination—he wished "to draw a little blood." On the second he arrives within twelve miles of the city, reaches Palmyra, and retraces his steps—do you say, reader to Pottawotomie? And, third, he is a mere looker on, and did no more, to say the least, than any of the hundred ladies who were engaged in making cartridges, or the two, certainly, who entered the trenches with tin pails of cartridges to aid their brothers in firing more rapidly, should occasion demand. And yet his eulogists tell us he was the "brave defender of Lawrence, and without his services the city would have been destroyed on these occasions."

At Bismark Grove, near Lawrence, Kansas, on the 16th of September, 1879, I heard a gentleman, from the platform, in the hearing of thousands of interested listeners, most of whom were comparatively new-comers in that State, make the broad and unqualified assertion that the freedom of Kansas was due to the services of Gen. Lane, and old John Brown. Shall they who *know* to the contrary, remain silent, and allow such statements to go down to another generation, and pass into history, uncontradicted? The most humble actual settler who located in Kansas with his family, who remained, and *voted* with the Free State party, rendered a greater service to freedom than did old John Brown, who never cast a vote there, and whose influence was to discourage Northern emigration, by his acts of violence. Gen. Lane is entitled to great credit for his services, and when I write of him I shall award him that credit he deserves. I write for another generation, with no expectation of reward, hence it is just that neither fear nor favor shall guide my pen.

AN INTERLUDE.

I have already stated that immediately after the 14th of September invasion, old John Brown and his sons, with their families, started overland, by way of Nebraska and Iowa, for the Eastern States. It is not my purpose to follow the Captain on his long journey; to detail the incidents by the way; his arrival in Chicago, in November; his efforts in Ohio to raise a regiment of men to march into Missouri to make reprisals; his visiting Albany in December; the particulars regarding his visit to his home and family at North Elba, Essex County, N. Y.; and thence to Boston, and visiting the Massachusetts Legislature in February, 1857. Neither is it my purpose to show his earnest efforts to raise funds to renew the strife in Kansas; his contract for pikes to arm the slaves in Missouri, where he was proposing to strike his next blow, but was finally diverted, by causes which shall appear in the sequel, to Harper's Ferry; his failures, vexations, disappointments, and denunciations of prominent Republicans, who stood in the way of his wild adventures, and who, he declared, were foes to the cause of freedom, because of their conservatism.

All the long period lying between September, 1856, and November, 1857, when the "Liberator" again returned to Kansas, was a period of almost unbroken rest, interrupted only by deep anxiety for the future, and the earnest discussions among Free State men as to the line of policy to be pursued, and which was crowned by wresting the Territorial Legislature from the bogus authorities, and sending a Free State Delegate to Congress. Save the Lecompton Constitution, which still endangered us, the question was virtually settled between freedom and slavery. A new era had dawned. A large emigration from the North began to flow in upon us. The timid, who had fled during the strife, had returned to their homes; the South were discouraged and had mostly fled; our Free State newspapers were revived; separated families were reunited; and in November, 1857, it needed no prophet's ken to settle the future that awaited disenthralled Kansas.

With this period of repose, I will introduce, with the consent of the reader, by way of interlude, a few sketches of border life, which I trust will not be wholly devoid of interest.

A STRANGE COINCIDENCE

By the generosity of those who were interested in the freedom of Kansas, and the personal efforts of Mrs. Brown, some $2,700 were contributed to aid in the revival of the *Herald of Freedom*. Much of this amount was reimbursed during the ensuing year. Less than $1,600 reached the writer of this, owing to large sums expended in defraying expenses of agents, and in a fruitless attempt to obtain, first from Judge McLean, at Cincinnati, and afterwards Judge Curtis, in Massachusetts, members of the Supreme Court of the United States, writs of *habeas corpus* for the relief of the treason prisoners.

During the summer of 1856, while still in durance, I opened a correspondence with the Cincinnati Type Foundry, for a duplication of the bills of the newspaper department of the office. That Company chanced to have a hand press, type and fixtures at Manhattan, which had been obtained of them by fraud, but possession had been regained before the boxes were opened. They sent me an order for the outfit, to Mr. Pipher, still living at Manhattan.

Immediately after my discharge from arrest I procured the services of Augustus Wattles, then living near Bloomington, Kan., who, with his teams, started by the way of Topeka for the goods.

Conscious of the great risk we were running, and the probabilities of capture by guerillas, on its way down to Lawrence, through the aid of a pro slavery friend, who was not in sympathy with the violent proceedings of his party, and in whose integrity I had implicit confidence, I had papers made out, putting the office in his hands, so that if captured by "Beford's men" it would revert e ss reach me safely.

Thus provided, Mr. Wattles, with the requisite order, obtained the material from Mr. Pipher, and set out on his return journey. When in the neighborhood of Silver Lake he was captured by a roving body of armed men. Not recognizing his captors he exhibited his pro slavery papers. The "boys" assured him that a press was just the thing they wanted. He was escorted to Topeka, where he revealed the truth, was recognized by acquaintances, and passed on to Lawrence, without further incident.

As Mr. Wattles passed up Massachusetts street, between Henry and Winthrop, with his teams, a body of mounted horsemen entered Massachusetts street from the ford of the river, *dragging in the dust behind them a red flag*, the identical one which waved over the *Herald of Freedom* office on the 21st of May previous, when it was destroyed by Border Ruffians. The new press and the captors of the flag met at the corner of Winthrop street, where the office was located.

The Free State boys, I do not remember under whose command, had captured the day previous, I think, near Easton, a company of South Carolinians, and took their flag and arms. The victors presented me with a musket, which they took from the vanquished, on the barrel of which was stamped the State arms, and the words "South Carolina," showing that the last of the original states admitted into the Union, had contributed from her State armory munitions of war for our subjugation. I regret to write that the musket was lost by some means in one of the Indian scares in Western Kansas, as I left it with A. R. Leonard, Esq., residing near Lawrence, to be forwarded to me in Illinois. I have the bayonet still

FURTHER STRATEGY.

Though I had succeeded in getting the necessary printing material I had no paper. Messrs. Younglove & Hoyt, of Cleveland, Ohio, donated me $200 in printing paper, soon after the office was destroyed. This was shipped to Alton, Ill., and remained in the warehouse there through the summer. I ordered it to be forwarded to Mr. McAllister, Lecompton, Kan., through a leading pro-slavery commission house in St. Louis, thence to the care of a *violent* one in Leavenworth. In due time Mr. McAllister was notified of its arrival at Leavenworth. He was Gov. Geary's private secretary. His given name is forgotten.

Mr. McAllister procured some pro-slavery teamsters at Lecompton, to haul the paper from Leavenworth, with instructions to cross the ferry at Lawrence, on their return. The teamsters received the paper from the warehouse, and returned homeward, no doubt congratulating themselves on the idea that they would now have a trusty Democratic paper again in operation at Lecompton.

Knowing about the time they would reach the river a watch was kept for them. On their arrival, on the Lawrence side, I presented them an order from McAllister to deliver the paper to me, which they did, but exhibited much chagrin and mortification in doing so

This is the manner, the first time made public, the Ruffians were circumvented, who had resolved that no Free State newspaper office or printing material should again be allowed to reach Kansas. Foiled in this, and the circulation of the *Herald of Freedom*, reaching 8,000 during the winter, they readily discovered the truth of the adage that "The blood of the martyrs is the seed of the church," and thought it best to not disturb the papers in the future.

AN EXCITING INCIDENT.

To illustrate the times and disturbed state of Kansas, during this interesting period in the history of the Territory, I give the following facts:

After our release from imprisonment; the arrival of Gov. Geary; the return of Gens. Heiskell and Reed, with their invading army of twenty-seven hundred to Missouri; the disappearance of old John Brown, his sons and their families towards Iowa; the arrest and imprisonment of Col. Harvey and his command of one hundred, who had unwisely responded to an "order" of Gen. Lane's, after Gov. Geary's proclamation of peace; and while Gov. Geary and his escort were making a tour of Southern Kansas to tranquilize the agitation in that quarter, probably sometime during the last days of October, I was sitting at my table, in the sanctum of the *Herald of Freedom* office building, preparing copy for the paper. A rap at the inner door. I arose, opened it, and saw three men standing before me, armed with revolvers and bowies, and I think Sharp's rifles. Speaking to them, one introduced himself as Captain H. Shaking hands with him, he then introduced the others, one as "my first Lieutenant," giving his name, which has escaped me; the other as "second Lieutenant," whose name is also forgotten. I passed them chairs, and took a seat myself at the table where I had been writing.

Capt. H. opened the conversation; inquired how soon the *Herald of Freedom* would again appear; congratulated me on my restoration to liberty, and then said, with a hearty laugh, in which the whole trio joined: "Gov. Geary is tranquilizing the Territory." I replied that he seemed doing much in that direction, and from the character of letters to me from personal friends in Pennsylvania, who knew Gov. Geary well, and from private intercourse with him, I had no doubt of his success, provided the authorities at Washington would not interfere with his work.

"He can never do it," replied Capt. H. "It is too late. The Ruffians have overrun Kansas, have had their day until the Free State men are thoroughly organized for revenge, and now they want to *tranquilize* us. Ha, ha, ha, they can't do it. Let me tell you, Mr. Brown, my Lieutenants here and myself have been following in the rear of Gov. Geary's pacific tour, and we have been trying to show that the thing won't tranquilize." He then proceeded to narrate various crimes they had committed, entering into details, telling of murders, arsons, *rapes*, horsestealing, and other offenses of an aggravated character.

I was wholly alone in the presence of three brutal ruffians. What should I do? I said:

"I think you mistake the true policy. Our ambition is to make Kansas a Free State. Our success is contingent upon the number of actual settlers we have from the free North, who will co-operate with us. To get these settlers it is our interest, as well as duty, to quiet down the excitement, show up the beauty of the country, the healthful climate, productive soil, and satisfy them that we have the ability to make it free, and we will see such an emigration Kansasward next spring as the world has never seen before. You must remember, Captain, that the great mass of us are here with our families, our property, with all we have in the world. We came here to build up homes and free institutions, and to be successful we must have peace and quiet."

"You can't do it. You can't do it. It is too late. We have got stirred up in the matter, and by G— we shall keep it stirred up. I have told you what we have done. We shall continue in the rear of Gov. Geary's movements, and we shall continue to agitate," replied the Captain, the Lieutenants with oaths endorsing his threats.

"Gentlemen, if this is the case, I shall feel in honor bound to repeat this conversation to Gov. Geary, and, much as I despise the bogus authorities, I shall hope to see you arrested and convicted for your crimes."

They all sprung to their feet, drew their revolvers, and threatened me with dire vengeance. I arose at the same instant, shoved a paper aside on the table, exposing an armory, which experience had taught me were good things to have on such occasions. Without showing fear I ordered them from the room; told them they would hear nothing further from me, unless I heard of further violence from them. They retreated down stairs, and twenty-two years have passed since then. Whether any of them are now living I don't know, but the facts are in every essential particular as I have narrated.

To the old settlers of Kansas I will make an explanation in this connection, and to the "Letter-Writers," an apology. In the summer of 1857, the letter-writers of which there were some thirteen or more, had headquarters at the Whitney House, in Lawrence. If any event was about to transpire, in any portion of the Territory, they would send one of their number to that point, who would gather up the facts, return to the general rendezvous, make his report, when each one would write his respective paper of the event, filling up with such incidents as an active imagination would suggest, and dating their letters at distant points. Thus, corroborated by each other in main facts, all was taken as true as holy writ. Indeed the Eastern press used the same arguments to show that they were truthful, as the vindicators of the bible have done to show the correctness of the sacred writers. "They were written at different times, by different persons, widely separated from each other, of cotemporary events, and all agree in main facts, therefore their statements are strictly reliable."

These letter writers were almost invariably sensational; the more exciting their narrations the greater the demand, and the more letters would be required. They generally received $5 each for their correspondence. The more letters they wrote the better it paid. The *Herald of Freedom* was ever correcting their statements, and trying to convince the eastern public that "bloody Kansas" was not half as bloody as the correspondents were representing. Something was necessary to protect the guild. A friend of mine, who had access to their rooms, reported that the whole list of Letter-Writers had entered into a solemn agreement to crush the *Herald of Freedom*, by representing the editor with having "sold out to the administration, gone over to the enemy." Remembering that Captain H. was then an eastern correspondent, whether of the guild I do not know, I unwisely stated the fact, in and editorial, that the letter writers had resolved to write down the *Herald of Freedom;* that we had corrected too many of their falsehoods through our columns for them longer to submit to it quietly; that they were not the sort of men whose truthfulness could be always relied upon; that one of their number was a professional horse thief, and he would be known because he had and would continue to write the most bitter things denunciatory of the *Herald of Freedom* and its editor. The insane man running through the streets stating that "Hell was out for noon," don't half express the excitement which that brief editorial caused among the scribling fraternity. I think a dozen challenges to fight duels followed in rapid succession, and the most dignified of them insisted on a correction as to him. Our statement was strictly true, but no doubt rather sweeping in its effect; and, looked upon from this distant stand point, more than 22 years after, we will say frankly, if his name does not commence with H. he was not *the* letter-writer to whom we referred, and, to save another challenge, we may as well mention that his name was not Hinton.

THE TERRIBLE FATE OF A TYPO.

While the foregoing incidents illustrate one phase of Kansas life, and show the disturbed state of the country, I will recite still another, as due to the faithful exposition of the times.

It was during this same autumn of 1856. With the destruction of the *Herald of Freedom* office, my own arrest and imprisonment, and business of every sort suspended throughout the Territory, my typos were thrown out of employment, and every honest means of support was cut off. Four months of the outer world shut out, I lost all trace of them, save of Mr. Whitcomb, who remained faithful to his trust, and did what he could to collect the broken and scattered ruins of one of the best printing offices ever taken to Kansas, and prevent further spiolation. He still lives in Lawrence, with his pleasant family, pursuing the delightful occupation of a florist.

At the time of this incident I had succeeded in getting our Free State citizen soldiery removed from the office building, who I found in full possession of each of the three floors, when I returned from camp; had received my new printing office, in spite of Border Ruffian vigilance, which had determined no new printing establishment should reach Free State men in the Territory, and had it arranged in place. My paper, too, had already come to hand, as before mentioned. In short, I was ready to resume work on the typographical department of the paper. Sitting in my sanctum, as in the preceding incident, preparing matter for publication, I heard a loud call at the door:

"Brown, O, Brown."

I stepped quickly to the door, and saw a tall, lank, awkward looking figure of the *genus homo*, sitting astride a fine horse, at the same time leading sixteen others, which were tied together by twos, then a long rope passing between them to which each pair of horses were fastened. The following colloquy ensued:

"Why, G," (I shall use only the initial, for reasons which appear in the sequel,) "is that you? I am so glad to see you," reaching up and shaking him by the hand. "Where have you been through the summer?"

"Well, lying around loose."

"I have frequently thought of you, and wondered why you did not put in an appearance. Everything is now in working order, and I am short of typos. I wish you to go to work immediately."

"I would like to oblige you, Mr. Brown, but I can't do it. Got something better."

"How is that?"

"Why, I have this stock to dispose of. Gov. Geary seems hell bent on tranquilizing things, and I am going to 'git' as fast as I can with this stock out of the Territory, and let him tranquilize."

"Where in the world did you get those horses?"

"They are reprisals which I have made for my last summer's work."

With a cordial shake, and "good bye," I saw G. for the last time riding hurriedly towards the ferry.

Fourteen years after I was at Fulton, Illinois, and in conversation with the publisher of the *Journal*, learned that it was established by himself and G., I think in the spring of 1857. As he mentioned the name, it being an odd one, I stated the above facts, with a description of G.'s person, and that he was a native Hoosier.

"You have described him accurately. He is the same person. I well remember his frequent mention of those bord'e troubles in Kansas."

"Had he any money to start with?"

"Yes, probably the proceeds of the sale of those horses."

"What has become of him?"

"I bought him out. He got religion, joined the Baptist church, and is now preaching over in Iowa."

"The Devil he is," is all I could respond. "And the proceeds of the stolen horses was the capital he commenced the ministry with."

Should this meet Rev. Mr. G.'s eye, he need not distress himself, for I shall not give the residue of the letters which spell his rather homely name, and I trust my friend Mr. Whitcomb will not. Nothing short of an inquisitorial rack, or thumb screw, at least, shall wring them from me; and I know Mr. Booth, late of the Fulton *Journal*, will not expose him, because he is a member of the same church.

BREWERTON.

Again a rap at the door of the *sanctum*, to which I responded. It could not have varied many days either way from the two preceding cases.

In stepped a rather pleasant looking, gentlemanly appearing person, some thirty years of age, and extended his hand. I said:

"You have the advantage of me."

"Don't you remember Brewerton, of the N. Y. *Herald?*"

"Yes, very well, you d—d scoundrel, and you get out of here this instant."

Standing back, as if perfectly shocked, he exclaimed:

"What does this mean."

"It means sir, that you are the d—d scoundrel who came to my room, at the Harris House, in Westport, with a lot of Southern desperadoes, while I was a prisoner in the hands of a mob, who exhibited a letter they represented they had taken from the carpet bag of some person from Lawrence, whom they claimed to have captured, revealing a plot to rescue me from them, and when I told them it was a forgery, put up by some person of evil intent, you, like the d—d scoundrel you are, labored to convince me and them that it was genuine, when you knew it was only a pretext, they were seeking, to take me out and shoot me, as they had repeatedly told me they would do to prevent a rescue."

"But, you know I was suspected, as a Northern man, and had to work my card very adroitly to keep on good terms with them, and save my own life, during that period of great excitement."

"Yes, you played the scoundrel and sneak to divert attention from yourself, and I want you to leave this office instantly."

"But I am not accustomed to being talked to in this manner. I was formerly a midshipman in the United States Navy."

"The greater reason why you should have been a gentleman. *Git!*"

And he got.

Reader, I always despised profane language and made it an invariable rule to discharge from my employ any workman accustomed to its use, or who was intemperate in the use of spirituous liquors, but in this case please remember our "Uncle Toby, in Flanders," who used to swear enormously big oaths while there, but when the recording angel had written down the words, and remembered the great occasion which called them forth, according to Sterne, he dropped a tear upon the record, and wiped it out forever. I trust he did so on the above occasion.

And then we have a somewhat analogous case with Uncle Toby's, which, with the reader's permission, I will offer in further extenuation. It was told me by a clergyman for the truth, and of course it is so.

Late in the autumn of 1854, so ran the story, an eastern settler, whom we will call Mallory, was engaged with his oxen in doing some labor just out of Lawrence. A clergyman riding past interrupted the laborer with:

"Good morning, Mr. Mallory."

"Good morning, Elder, I am glad to see you."

"But I was not aware until this morning that you were a profane man."

"I am not, I never swear. My parents were pious people, and they gave me a pious education. I always despised the practice of profane swearing."

"You surprise me, Mr. Mallory. I cannot understand it. As I came up I thought I never heard a person swear so wickedly as you were doing."

"Oh, no, Elder, your ears have deceived you. I *never* swear."

"How could I be so deceived?"

"Why, what in the world could I have

said that you have mistaken it for profanity?"

"You were directing your remarks to the oxen."

"Oh, oh, Elder, I understand you now. The truth is, I bought these cattle down in Missouri, and I was only addressing language to them they would understand."

It is hoped the people of Lawrence have ceased to buy Missouri cattle; and if Brewerton never intrudes himself again on my premises, I will *try* and never use such emphatic terms again.

A FIRST CLASS BORE.

Bores are frequent attendants in a newspaper office. They thoughtlessly trespass on the time and patience of the editor, when he is preparing important matter for the press, delay the printers, by forcing them to wait for copy, and annoy him in all sorts of ways. I have a case of this character, which the reader will allow me to narrate, for the benefit of the press, which, certainly is applicable to our title of a "Thrilling Incident of Border Life."

It was December, 6th 1856. The day was rather cheerless. Moist snow was falling in large flakes, melting nearly as soon as it reached the ground.

I was seated in my sanctum, as usual, hard at work, writing editorials for my paper, which then had a circulation bordering closely on 8,000. I had no assistant, and often wrote from ten to sixteen columns of matter each week, besides conducting a heavy business correspondence. To do this vast amount of labor I was compelled to be wholly alone. My clerks were instructed to allow no person to pass through their room into mine, unless it was a case of the greatest importance.

The sanctum was a beautiful room, in the middle of the building, on the second floor, sixteen feet square, high ceiling, well lighted, the floor carpeted, two fine book cases well filled, pictures on the wall, a large round table in the center of the room, and a beautifully ornamented stove, which I took great pride in keeping nicely polished. In one corner of the room was a little trap door, probably 12 by 20 inches, a series of them extending through the building to the roof, to be used in cases of emergency. These traps gave direct access to the workmen, either on the first or third floor. The typos were above, and through the trap the foreman received his copy.

I was seated at my table, in the midst of a heavy article, laboring to show that tranquility was fully restored to Kansas; that the golden age had really dawned; that the lost Eden was found; our gorgeous prairies were teeming with honey and wine; and was telling everybody and his wife to come right there, by first steamer up the Missouri, and enjoy this newly-discovered Paradise, when I was interrupted by an attempt to enter at the door, which was fastened. I was in an unusual hurry, behind with copy, and a long train of thought, which I wished to get on paper, before it should take wings and fly away, as my best always does.

Two or three clerks, among whom, by the way, was John E. Cook, an accomplished penman, who was hung with old John Brown, at Harper's Ferry, were hard at work arranging subscription books in the business office, so I resolved I would not be interrupted.

But the door was shook again, followed by three raps, the sesame which had been agreed upon with the clerks to open the door.

Impatient with the annoyance, I passed to the door and opened it, when in stepped a gentleman of probably 35 years of age, heavy set, wearing a slouch hat, face unshaven for a week, with the general air of a man that had his own notion of things, and cared but little what others thought about it.

I passed him a chair, in front of the warm stove, made some remarks about the weather, when the following colloquy ensued:

"Rather an unpleasant day to travel."

"Quite."

"You have just arrived in the Territory?"

"Yes."

"Do you come to locate with us?"

"Yes."

"What State are you from?"

"Indiana."

"How are you pleased with Kansas?"

"Well."

Here the trap was raised, and the foreman called, "Copy."

"Excuse me a few minutes, I have an article well under way, which I will soon finish."

The trap was let down, when I dipped my pen, already between my fingers, in the ink, and remarked:

"I am very much pressed to supply copy as fast as needed, as my paper is almost wholly original."

Again I dipped my pen in the ink, as if to write, but my thoughts were gone. To add to my grief, my visitor took from his pocket a case of tobacco, extracted a quid, and commenced chewing, and soon after made a target of my beautiful stove. The door was open in front, exposing a glowing fire. He evidently aimed to hit the opening; but in spite of his skill in that direction he would frequently miss, then a hiss, accompanied by a foul odor, and a soiled place was exposed.

I tried to draw my visitor out, and learn the object of his call, but could not. Everything I said, or inquiry made, was answered with a monosyllable.

Up again, every few minutes, would fly the trap, and down would come the cry of "Copy! We are *all* out of copy."

The pen would be again loaded, but the thoughts were on the *bore*, and I could not write. To demand his business seemed impolite, and what to do was the conundrum I did not know how to solve. Dear reader, were you *ever* similarly afflicted?

Then it seemed an age. Looking back upon the events, and recalling the vexation I experienced at the abuse my stove was receiving, when I had long ago pushed a spittoon to my visitor's feet, to which he paid no attention, it is a wonder that I did not make a slight draft on Mallory's language to the oxen to help me out.

When my patience was nearly exhausted, and I was studying what to say to get rid of the intruder, to relieve the monotony, he arose, looked at the pictures on the wall, read my certificate of membership in the Grand Division Sons of Temperance, as also of the Grand Temple of Honor of Pennsylvania. Then coming to the table, with both hands on it, leaning over towards me, he inquired:

"Have you any subscribers at Centreville, Indiana?"

"I think so."

"Who are they?"

I stepped to the business room, called for my Indiana subscription book, opened to Centreville, and read a handsome list of names.

"Put down —"

I did so.

"Put down —"

"Put down —"

And so he continued, I following directions until I had added some eighteen names.

"Put down the number on a slip of paper. Have you any subscribers at Cedarville?"

"Yes."

"Who are they?"

And thus on from one place to another, each with a long list, until I had entered an even ninety names.

"How much do you want for them?"

"One hundred and thirty-five dollars I furnish them all to you at my lowest club rates."

He drew from his pocket a bag of coin, and counted out $135 in gold, which I transferred to my safe, *thinking* to myself as I did so:

"You may spit on my stove just as much as you dum please."

I then inquired his name. He gave it as Dr. Jas. G. Blunt. He was afterward Maj. General, in the war of the rebellion, and I had the pleasure of telling Col. Thomas Moonlight, now of Leavenworth, the above facts, in the presence of Gen. Blunt and several members of his staff.

I suppose my journalistic friends will call the General a "First Class Bore." While recently in Kansas, I learned with much sadness, that Gen. Blunt is at this time an inmate of an insane asylum, I think at Washington.

THE LETTER WRITERS.

Having had frequent occasion to refer to, or quote from the professional letter writers of Kansas, it may not be improper to give a few passing lines to them, before we return to the "Liberator." Many of the names of these gentlemen have escaped me. The most prominent were Jas. Redpath, Wm. Phillips, Richard Raelf, Richard J. Hinton, J. H Kagi and John E. Cook. There were others, as A. D. Richardson, Capt. H., previously mentioned, S. F. Tappan, Mr. Russel, etc. The first four names were foreigners, and nearly all were in sympathy with old John Brown, and acted as apologists, and vindicators of him.

Redpath made his first appearance in Kansas, in June, 1855. For a time he made his headquarters at the *Herald of Freedom* office, and I saw and knew much of him. He was ambitious to secure a position as reporter of the Bogus Legislature, which assembled at Pawnee on the 2nd of July, 1855, and was successful. He failed, for some reason, to give satisfaction, and was discharged, after the removal of that body to the Shawnee Mission. He claimed to have traveled all over the South, mostly on foot, spending much of his time among the slaves. As a correspondent he was wholly unreliable, drawing so largely on his imagination that it was difficult to distinguish the truth from falsehood. He was a violent Northern secessionist in feeling, and all his energies seemed directed to involve the extremes of the Republic in a bloody collision. He established a paper at Doniphan, under the auspices of Gen. Lane, but they soon fell out, and he left the Territory in disgust, and engaged in the Haytian emigration business. To aid the enterprise he published a paper at Boston, entitled the *Palm and Pine*, from which I have already copied. He is now the recognized head of the Boston Literary Bureau. He recently disappeared mysteriously from New York, but in due time turned up in San Francisco.

Mr. Phillips was sent to Kansas as the special correspondent of the New York *Tribune*, in the summer or autumn of 1855. He was a man of fine ability, designed to write nothing but the truth, and had many excellent qualifications of head and heart. He placed too much confidence in the reports of his associates; frequently magnified molehills into mountains; and was an extreme partizan with a tendency toward the John Brown school. Instead of encouraging Northern emigration, his published articles were always lugubrious and lacking in hope and confidence in the final result.

Richard Raelf came to Kansas, overland, through Iowa, in the fall of 1856, reaching Lawrence with the Eldridge party, some time about the middle of October. Raelf represented himself as an adopted son of Lady Byron; claimed to have had some trouble with her; came to New York, and engaged as an assistant to Mr Pease, in the House of Industry, belonging to the Five Point's Mission. Thence he drifted to Kansas. He was "something of a poet," an enthusiastic admirer of old John Brown, an advocate of the fighting policy, but was not a success as a correspondent. He suicided last year in San Francisco.

Hinton, like Redpath, Philips and Raelf, was an Englishman. He came to Kansas with the same party with Raelf, in October, 1856. He obtained a situation as typo, in the *Herald of Freedom* office, but was wholly incompetent as a compositor, being paid by the thousand, his wages rarely or never exceeded $3 50 a week, when good workmen made $12 to $15 a week. He was transferred to the position of assistant clerk, and thence joined the letter-writing fraternity.

Cook, too, was an employe for some three months in the *Herald of Freedom* office; was engaged principally in copying subscription books; making indexes; and entering lists of new subscribers. He came to Kansas in the spring of 1856, from Indiana, and joined Lenhart and others in a sort of guerilla warfare through that summer. He fell into the embraces of old John Brown, and died on the gallows a few days after the "Liberator." He was a man of generous impulses, and, in peaceful times, and other surroundings would have made a worthy citizen. An anonymous writer, since these articles were in course of publication, wrote me that he lacked bravery.

Kagi I never saw but once, and then was favorably impressed with his appearance. He was correspondent for the *National Era*, at Washington, a very worthy, high-toned, Free Soil paper. He was Captain Brown's Secretary of War, and was killed at Harper's Ferry. He became known in Kansas principally by a personal encounter with Judge Elmore, at Tecumseh.

These young men, inexperienced in practical life, imbued with the wildest romance, and seeking to involve the Government in revolution, writing under *nom de plumes*, and flooding the country with sensational letters, in too many instances wholly devoid of truth, gave a false coloring to history, which will probably impress it for years, if not for all time. Take the "Life of John Brown," written by one of them, for illustration: I have shown conclusively that the production is in no way reliable; that the entire work was a eulogy published in the interest of John Brown's family, with everything objectionable in his character carefully omitted, or heavily gilded; and yet so worthy and enduring a work as "The American Cyclopedia," in its article on Old John Brown, has only greatly abridged Redpath's book, without adding a single additional statement. Probably the Encyclopedia Britanica borrows its article, in substance, from the American. French and German publications will follow, while other nations will copy, and thus is realized the truth of that maxim: "Falsehood will travel a league while Truth is putting on his boots to join in pursuit."

Sensational writers, endorsing each other, gave coloring to everything they attempted. Genuine merit was obscured and real worth was passed without mention; tinsel was thrown over their heroes, whilst their meritorious works were magnified many times, and their vices and crimes concealed. Thus left, the future historian has a herculean task before him, else an admiring generation will convert these heroes of an idle

Exeunt, the letter writers.

JOHN BROWN'S CABIN—A FRAUD.

Hon. James Hanway, of Lane, Franklin Co., Kansas, at the Old Settlers' Convention, at Bismark Grove, near Lawrence, on the 15th and 16th of September, 1879, said, from the public stand, that he wished to make a correction in regard to old John Brown, because it was due to history. He then said a photographer had taken a picture of an old log cabin, which he had erected on his place at an early day, for preemption purposes, but had long been unoccupied. After the picture was complete the artist inquired what he should call it.

"Well, old John Brown used to visit me quite frequently, while we lived in the cabin, suppose we call it the 'John Brown Cabin.'"

Agreeably to the suggestion, Judge Hanway said, the picture was so named, and the artist went away with it. A little time after he saw an engraved illustration of the cabin, in a Kansas City paper, and published as the veritable John Brown's Cabin. At the Philadelphia Centennial, the old gentleman added, there were thousands of this fraud disposed of to the credulous, at high figures, who wanted some relic of their hero. "But John Brown," he continued, "never owned a cabin nor any land in Kansas."

In the first biennial report of the State Board of Agriculture of Kansas, a beautifully executed volume of 632 pages printed on heavy paper, and finely illustrated, we find a wood cut of this cabin fraud, so characteristic of many other events Brown's eulogists have falsely heaped upon him, for the historian to correct, underneath which is printed "John Brown's Cabin, in southwestern part of Franklin county, near Osawotomie, Miami Co., (from a photograph by A. W. Barker.)"

Gov. Anthony aided and abetted in extending and perpetuating this fraud, by sending a copy of the engraving to a Subscription Club in Paris, France. He says: "With this I hand you an engraving of 'John Brown's Cabin,' still standing, as it did when it domiciled the old hero during his residence in Kansas."

This fact shows how myths are made. That cabin will be as immortal as the apple in the mythical story of Wm. Tell. Are all our histories of prominent personages as devoid of truth as are those of old John Brown?

THE HOME OF JOHN BROWN.

From the same piece with the "Cabin Fraud" comes a statement as late as November 12, 1879, from the present Governor of Kansas, John P. St John, a very excellent gentleman, by the way, who telegraphed the Chicago *Daily News*, as the Governor said, from "The home of Old John Brown."

Seven cities claimed to be the birthplace of Homer; but it is difficult to understand how it is possible for any person, while living, to have two "homes" at the same time. "Home," in law and fact, is the place where a person is domiciled. Domicile is a place of *permanent* residence. That place is where the family resides. From John Brown's first entrance into Kansas, in the fall of 1855, to the time of his execution, December 2d, 1859, his family was on his farm at North Elba, New York, and there, in the writer's natal county of Essex, among the Adirondac mountains, where he was born, rests in tranquility the bones of the "Liberator." Far be it from me to disturb his repose, or wrest from his fame a single well-earned laurel; but I am laboring to brush away the false in history, which his eulogists have thrown around him, in many instances robbed from those better entitled to wear the garland than he.

A GLANCE IN PASSING.

Many of the most interesting pages in Kansas history, when correctly and fully written, will be those describing the intervening events between the autumn of 1856, and November, 1857. The period embraces the whole of Gov. Geary's administration, extending through six months; of Secretary Stanton's term, as Acting Governor, for one month; and about six months of Gov. Walker's administration.

The correspondents and "fighting men," made a continual warfare on these gentlemen; but they were, nevertheless, very worthy persons, and came to Kansas with a sincere desire to do justly by all parties. They were hampered by instructions issued by the State Department at Washington, and were frequently embarassed with interferences by co-ordinate departments of government. Each employed all his power to correct abuses, and continually labored with the President in that direction, but was unsuccessful.

The President was under the influence of Jefferson Davis, the man of "evil destiny," who seemed to have Kansas affairs in his keeping, and whose great ambition was to make it a slave State.

When Gov. Geary saw he could not be permitted to right our wrongs, he resigned, and left the Territory; but his influence for free Kansas did not end here. After Gov. Walker's appointment he paid that functionary a visit, and made known to him the outrages which had been perpetrated on the Free State settlers, by Missouri and the South, and placed him in rapport with influential Free State men in Kansas, who wielded valuable influence over him during his whole term of office.

When Gov. Walker found that his instructions would not permit a faithful discharge of his duties to the citizens, he visited Washington in person, and labored with the President to get his instructions changed; failing, he, too, resigned.

Secretary Stanton, who again became Acting Governor, also attempted to assist the real settlers, but was immediately sacrificed to placate the South, and was removed by the President.

Each of the Governors were violently denounced by the Bohemians of the press, and with Gov. Walker, it required great effort to prevent his being driven into extreme measures, by their false, abusive and violent denunciations of him.

Each of these Governors, on leaving the Territory, became indentified with the friends of free Kansas. Gov. Geary served his country with gallantry in the war of the rebellion, and was made Governor of Pennsylvania, by the Republican party, discharging his duties faithfully and satisfactorily to all. Gov. Walker was sent by President Lincoln, on a secret and very important mission to England, during the rebellion, and received therefor the highest commendation of the Martyr President. These facts show that however greatly they were misunderstood the time, in Kansas, their impulses were leading them in a proper direction.

The writer had special opportunities of information in regard to the official conduct of each of these gentlemen; and he believes it a duty he owes to impartial history, some day, to give that knowledge to the public.

In my next I shall resume John Brown's connection with Kansas affairs, and hurry these Reminiscences to a close, stopping by the way, to correct any erros, pointed out by critics, which, lapse of years, or defective information has led me into. Each person who has or may point out any discrepancy between my statements and facts will please accept my cordial thanks.

RETURN TO KANSAS.

During this long period, from about the middle of September, 1856, to November, 1857, old John Brown has been laboring in the Eastern States, soliciting funds to arm a body of men to return to Kansas, and make reprisals in Missouri. As before stated, he contracted in Collinsville, Conn., for one thousand pikes, to be "fixed to the end of a pole, about six feet long," which he told the manufacturer he proposed "to place in the hands of the settlers in Kansas, to keep in their cabins, to defend themselves against 'border ruffians and wild beasts.'" This was his *ostensible* object. His REAL object was to place these rude instruments, which only required physical force to wield them, in the hands of slaves in Missouri.

In August, 1857, Capt Brown, with a small party, reached Tabor, near the south-western corner of Iowa, where he remained inactive until the 2d of November, when, with one of his sons, he set out with his own conveyance for Kansas. We find him a few days after in council with various parties in the vicinity of Lawrence. His stay in that vicinity was quite brief, limited to about three days. He seems to have enlisted John E. Cook, Richard Realf and L. F. Parsons in his enterprise on this trip. Redpath was already co-operating, and Hinton, according to Cook, was to have joined the adventure. The Captain returned by way of Topeka, to Nebraska, thence to his place of general rendezvous, at Tabor.

Why the Captain made so brief a stay in Kansas is not apparent. Probably he was disappointed in finding that the "Voting Policy," as distinguished from the "Fighting Policy," had prevailed.

Certain it is, the Free State party, through the faithfulness of Gov. Walker to public and private pledges, had control of both houses of the Legislative Assembly of the Territory, and had secured the certificate of election for their Delegate in Congress. This matter hung in doubt for a time, and the Bohemians of the press were almost positive in their statements that Gov. Walker and Secretary Stanton would play false to their pledges.

It is *possible* the Captain's movement was inspired Kansasward at that time, with a bloody project in view. It was certainly fortunate for the tranquility of the Territory that he was detained in Iowa, from the 7th of August to the 2d of November "for the want of funds," as his biographer states, for it is very probable a renewal of strife was saved by the event.

I have one of the most exciting chapters in Kansas history, to detail, *sometime*, which occurred during this interesting period, and which may partially explain John Brown's reasons for hovering on the borders of Kansas during this interval. To introduce it in these pages would require the introduction of other characters, which are not at present the subjects of inquiry, hence an account of it is reserved for another occasion.

Each movement of the Captain, until his visit in November to Lawrence, looked towards a renewal of the strife by him on the Kansas border. He had bid "farewell" to New England in April, 1857; had an engagement with Col. Hugh Forbes to meet him at Tabor in June to instruct a number of young Kansas men in military tactics; in May he was journeying in that direction. On July 4th he left Cleveland, O., for Iowa City. Reached Tabor on the 7th of August. Was joined by his "drill master" on the 9th. He had quite a little party with him at this time. He visited Lawrence in November, as we have just seen, taking one son with him, and leaving two others at Tabor. He called on E. B. Whitman, living a few miles west of Lawrence. On reaching Topeka, *en route* back to Tabor, he told Cook that the party "were to leave Kansas to attend a military school during the winter; and that it was the intention to go to Ashtabula County, Ohio."

Now it seems there was a sudden change in the "Liberator's" mind. Here is a back step, and an explanation as to the cause is required. On his return to Tabor he communicated to his followers that Harper's Ferry would be the point of attack.

Did the Captain call on Gov. Robinson while in Lawrence? What was the character of their interview? Did that interview have anything to do with his change of base, and his precipitate retreat? I have written the Governor for information in this direction, and hope to receive his answer in time for the next number of the series.

AN IMPORTANT LETTER.

I wrote Gov. Robinson recently, as stated in the previous article, recalling a conversation between us twenty years ago, in regard to an interview between him and Old John Brown, and wished the facts for publication. He hesitated to furnish a statement, but with the assurance that I should repeat it according to my recollections, which would possibly bring him before the public in reply, he sent me the following, which has just reached me in time for this place. Whether that interview was had on the occasion of the Captain's visit to Lawrence, in November, 1857, when his whole plan of operations seemed so suddenly changed, or a year later, at the close of the troubles in Linn and Bourbon Counties, is not apparent. From some facts in my possession I am led to think it occurred on the occasion of this visit, for the Governor saw clearly the end of civil strife at that time, and, like other permanent settlers who desired to see order substituted for anarchy, was laboring to bring about an era of peace. It is possible the Captain's mission was in pursuit of money with which to prolong the agitation, and which the Governor thought best to withhold from him, at the same time suggesting very good reasons for so doing. But these, the reader will understand, are my own deductions. The letter is as follows:

LAWRENCE, Kan., Nov. 24, 1879.

GEO. W. BROWN, M. D.—DEAR SIR:— Your favor asking for an account of my interview with John Brown, as he left the Territory of Kansas, is received. The particulars of the conversation I cannot give, as I made no memoranda at the time. The interview was very friendly, and a frank review was had of the two lines of policy pursued in Kansas, namely, his policy of involving the North and South in a war; and our Free State policy of surrounding the slave States with free, and securing the Federal as well as State governments on the side of freedom.

He frankly admitted that from my standpoint we had acted wisely, and had succeeded; but from his standpoint, so far as aiding the cause of emancipation, it was a failure. But as his presence here would be a source of annoyance, and do no good, he would seek another field of operations, but did not say where.

It may not be generally known that I was authorized to draw on a person in Boston, for money to support John Brown in Kansas, if I thought his presence beneficial to the Free State cause. I had written this person that I thought his presence a hindrance rather than a help at that time. Probably Mr. Brown had been so informed. It is possible that Amos A. Lawrence can tell where the letter can be found.

I notice in Redpath's book, he represents Mr. Brown as speaking very contemptuously of the Free State men in general, and of myself in particular. If so he was very hypocritical, as in my presence he was always most respectful, and appeared to give Free State men credit for acting honestly and efficiently, although not to suit him or his policy.

Very truly, C. ROBINSON.

Whether this interview was in the autumn of 1857 or 1858, is not important to these inquiries. It shows how the Governor regarded the prolongation of civil strife, and how sincerely desirous he was to end it. And it gives us, in his own words, what he thought of John Brown's services in Kansas as an auxiliary in the cause of freedom.

"KANSAS TOO HOT FOR HIM"

Another interesting period in Kansas history is passed, lying between the middle of November, 1857, to the last of June, 1858, when our hero again appears upon the scene. There had been more or less difficulty for some months, in southern Kansas, growing out of conflicting land titles between Free State and pro-slavery men. This led to aggressive acts on the part of each of the contending factions.

A party of armed pro-slavery ruffians, sometime in June, 1858, under the leadership of one Hamilton, visited a Free State neighborhood, and gathered one by one, eleven citizens, marched them into a deep ravine, formed them into line, and fired upon them. They all fell to the ground, five were instantly killed, five were seriously wounded, and one escaped unharmed.

An intense excitement justly followed this bloody procedure. The whole country was on fire. Capt Brown was in the States at the time, had just made arrangements for the completion of his pikes in Connecticut, and for their shipment to Chambersburgh, Pa., on their way to Virginia. He again hurried to Kansas, taking his faithful Kagi with him. According to Redpath, one of the motives which prompted Captain Brown to return to Kansas, at this time, was to divert attention from his Harper's Ferry project. On his return to Iowa, in '57, from Lawrence, he had freely communicated to Col. Forbes, his drill master, his changed plan of operations. During the winter they fell out, and Forbes left for the East. The Captain was fearful that the Colonel would communicate to the government his plan of operating in Virginia, hence his appearance in Kansas, the Marias des Cygnes massacre furnishing an excuse, to disguise his real purpose. From that time until the close of 1858, civil strife, with all its horrors, raged in the counties of Linn and Bourbon, which bordered on Missouri.

Neighbor was arrayed against neighbor, and each party sought the destruction of the other. Conservative Free State men and pro-slavery men united and tried to allay the excitement. The result was their being indiscriminately pillaged by each party. Crimination and re-crimination was the order of the day. Though the disturbance was originally began by the pro-slavery agitators, the violence of Hamilton met with earnest hostility from his own party friends, and many joined the conservative Free State men in trying to suppress the discord.

The reader would not be interested in a reviewal and detailed history of these exciting times. And I am frank to own that I have not the requisite knowledge to a clear exposition of them. Neither can I tell what important part John Brown played in them, other than he was associated with the extreme Free State men in making reprisals from the opposing factions.

The *Herald of Freedom* was regularly issued during this period, and correspondents were continually reporting the condition of affairs, but the statements were so conflicting that it seemed almost impossible to arrive at the truth.

It was during this period that the "Jayhawking" fraternity sprang into being, and such men as Quantrell, who at that time was recognized as a Free State man coming originally from Ohio, was educated for the terrible work he was afterwards guilty of, in leading a large party, [I was about to say five hundred, but apprehensive that John Speer, or some other critic, had counted them, and found there were but four hundred and ninety-nine, I have concluded to be extremely cautious,] of Bushwhackers into Lawrence, and shooting down in cold blood one hundred and eighty citizens, robbed the banks, pillaged the town, and burned the best portion of it, leaving ruin, desolation and death everywhere. It was a fearful school, and the consequences were not limited to a few years, nor confined to Kansas.

Brown made repeated raids into Missouri captured horses, "blooded stock," ran off slaves, and made his name a terror through all that region. The Governor of Missouri offered a reward of $3,000 for his apprehension, and made a requisition on the Governor of Kansas for his arrest and extradition as a fugitive from justice. President Buchanan added to the reward.

Gov. Denver, some time during this agitation, called to his aid Gov. Robinson, who had the confidence of the Free State men, and they, in company, visited the infected region, held public meetings, and labored with their respective friends to restore tranquility to the disturbed country. The United States District Court, Judge Elmore presiding, impaneled a Grand Jury, and subpœnaed a hundred or more witnesses, and called them to Lawrence to give evidence with a view to indictments.

While the Court was yet in session, the Legislature passed a general amnesty law; the Grand Jury was discharged; the witnesses returned to their homes; and quiet was restored to the convulsed border.

The American Cyclopedia says:—"Not only was a reward offered for Brown's arrest, but *the more moderate Free State men hastened to disavow any sympathy with his daring acts.* The Territory became TOO HOT FOR HIM, and he started, early in January, 1859, for the North, accompanied by four white companions and the liberated negroes."

Since then, save the troubles growing out of the rebellion, and the excesses produced by bad men educated to deeds of violence in these exciting times, many of whom, it is presumed, have paid the penalty for their wrongs in the penitentiary, and an occasional Indian scare on the Western border, general tranquility has prevailed throughout Kansas. The Lecompton Constitution was defeated; a State Constitution, by the honest settlers, was made, and the new State in due time became a member of the Federal Union with the motto on its seal of "*Ad astra per aspera*," [To the Stars through difficulties,] and the future prosperity of the State was secured.

EXAGGERATIONS OF HIS EULOGISTS.

The eastern press, and the eulogists of John Brown, were not content to make him a model hero, in almost every direction, but they gave him credit for fighting bravery where battles were never fought; they made him a leader where he did not command; they represented him a veteran warrior in battles fought while he was a stripling of fourteen years, and full eight hundred miles from the battle field; they gave him command of troops where there were none to fight; defended a town against a heavy invading force where every one fled to the brush; said he was the savior of a city, where the enemy did not fire a gun; they represented him as possessing wisdom he did not exhibit; with judgment to which he seemed a stranger; with owning cabins in which he was only a visitor; with being a grower of blooded stock, to put it mildly, which he *pressed* from their owners; with being a heavy landed proprietor in Kansas, where he never owned a rood; with having a home in Kansas when it was in north-eastern New York; claimed that his wife was insulted and abused, when she was more than a thousand miles distant from the place of pretended outrage; that he had a son hacked to pieces by a hatchet, whom it is questionable if he ever saw or heard of him until after his death.

Even the portraits exhibited by the admirers of old John Brown are *frauds*. During the whole period he was known in Kansas he wore a long, flowing beard. And the same was true of him, at the time of his execution; but the pictures his friends take delight in, were those of a man several years younger, with a smooth shaven face — probably John Brown, the wool-buyer; certainly not John Brown, the Guerilla Chieftain.

They credited him with making Kansas a Free State, whereas he retarded its prosperity and threw obstacles in the way of its most zealous and effective workers. Every slave he aided in escaping from Missouri; every horse pressed into his service; and every injury inflicted upon pro-slavery men was repeated on Free State men, by friends of the injured party, with compound interest.

Not content with all these, and numberless other misrepresentations of a similar character, they next gave him a residence in Osawotomie, where he only lived at times in the guise of a visitor with his sister, or other friends; and, to crown all, gave him a title *robber* from another. And that shall be the subject of my next sub-division.

OSAWOTOMIE BROWN.

Osawotomie lies near the junction of the Marias des Cygnes and Potawotomie creeks. Uniting at this point 'the river below is known as the Osage.

The town was located early in the spring of 1855, by S. C. Pomeroy, representing the N. E. Emigrant Aid Company, and Orville C. Brown, a lawyer from Utica, N. Y. The name of the town was compounded by dropping the last two letters from Osage, and the first five from Pottawotomie, joining, formed Osawotomie, with but one s, as here printed. [O-sa-wot-o-mie.]

Mr. Brown usually employed only his initials in writing his individual name. As there were so many other Browns in Kansas, and as Orville became quite prominent in our early conventions, he was frequently referred to and known at Lawrence, and elsewhere, as Osawotomie Brown. I recollect very well the earnestness he exhibited when arrested by the mob at Kansas City in place of the writer, and his protest that he was not the Brown they wanted. He was taken to Riddlesbarger's for identity, discharged, and then the renewal of the effort to take the "undersigned."

When Osawotomie was invaded by Missouri, in a fruitless attempt to capture old John Brown, for the Pottawotomie murders, a son of Orville, aged fourteen, fell into the hands of the marauders and was carried into Missouri. After a painful search he was found at Lexington, in the care of a Presbyterian deacon, who gladly restored him to his almost frantic parents. From about this time I lose sight of "the genuine, original and simon pure" Osawotomie Brown. Two years later we find the Eastern press applying the pseudonym of "Osawotomic" to old John Brown, the man whose "soul is marching on."

The press also confounded the name of R. P. Brown, mistaking him for a son of old John, whereas he was a teacher from Michigan, engaged professionally for a period in Mississippi. Seeing a negro burned alive in that State, for some trifling offense, as he told the writer, he left the South in great disgust, came to Kansas, and located near Leavenworth. He incurred the displeasure of some drunken pro-slavery ruffians, because of his intelligence, coolness and intrepidity in defense of his Free State neighbors, was set upon about the middle of January, 1856, and was struck several times on the head with the sharp edge of a hatchet, by which his skull was fractured. He was then thrown into a lumber wagon, taken home, and brutally dragged into the yard, where he died soon after, living long enough to say, "They have murdered me like a dog." It was a terrible affair, and the actors in the tragedy deserved a dozen deaths; but he and old John Brown were strangers, unless they became acquainted during the so-called "Wakarusa War."

NOT ALL BAD.

I am not writing a "biography of John Brown," nor a "History of Kansas," as my critics allege; but "Reminiscences," or recollections, as the word is defined, of the Captain, with "Incidents" or sketches of those times. Neither am I laboring to make my hero a monster of iniquity on the one hand, or a saint on the other. I have desired to tell only what I knew of him, and what has come to me, and which I believed, from others.

The Captain and the writer differed widely as regards the *means* to be employed to prevent the extension and secure the final extinction of slavery, as upon many other subjects. From my earliest recollection war seemed to me a terrible calamity. History was never a source of delight, because it was mostly detailed accounts of bloodshed and violence. I always thought there was no necessity for the arbitrament of the sword; that the differences between individuals, States and nations ought to find a solution in peaceful means. The God I reverenced was a tender Parent, ever seeking the elevation and happiness of his creatures, never their degradation.

The shedding of human blood, in my humble estimation, is never justifiable save in defense of life, or when it cannot be otherwise avoided. Capt. Brown's oft-quoted expression, "Without the shedding of blood there is no remission," seemed to give character to all the latter years of his life. He was a friend of the oppressed; with enlarged sympathies; a praying man; and, in many respects, no doubt, a good man; but with his peculiar organization, and his earnest desire to aid the poor slave, he did not properly take into consideration the condition, nor properly respect the rights, liberty and person of the master.

Like the "Liberator," I was an anti-slavery man; an abolitionist; a Free Soiler of the John Quincy Adams and J. R. Giddings school; but in going to Kansas I proposed to fight the battles of freedom on that plane which I believed would ensure success, and make that territory, and all others bordering upon it, free territory. "One thing at a time" has always seemed an excellent maxim. By occupying certain positions we could obtain such assistance as to insure the results we aimed at; while an opposite one would, no doubt, have driven thousands from us. I was opposed to what was known as the "black laws," and so were nearly if not all from the New England and Middle States. The Western pioneers, and the great mass, if not all who acted with us from the South, on the contrary, were Free State men only on the condition that negroes should be prohibited from settling among us. We of the East and North felt the terrible injustice of such a provision, and labored against it until we saw we were endangering everything by our persistency; then we subordinated our feelings to the prejudices of the masses, and remained silent, confident that more enlarged views would ultimately prevail, when we could regain what was temporarily lost.

John Brown, on the contrary, was firm and unbending. He conceded that his course had driven many, otherwise friends, into the opposition; still he kept on, determined to yield nothing for success. By so doing, but for others, we must have lost all.

That John Brown had many traits of character which commended him to the admiration of the public I am well aware. When on his way to the gallows he stooped and kissed a black child, a poor creature doomed, so far as the world then knew, to a life of toil and bondage. This incident aroused our tenderest sympathy. That act did much to redeem his past wrongs; but is no reason why we should cover him all over with adulation, falsifying history, and rob other men of their merits, to make him appear more sublime. I was willing to give him more than the benefit of a doubt, and admit that—in all his demands for "blood," when he was so anxious to "go out and draw a little" at Lawrence, from the invaders; when sending word to Gen. Lane that he would not obey another order unless it was to fight; his statement to Stearns that it would require a God to take Lecompte out of his hands if he had caught him; his whole life in Kansas, one of blood—he was partly insane—a monomaniac on the subject of slavery; a religious enthusiast, if the reader prefers, thinking that he was an instrument in the hands of God to wipe out American slavery.

It may be said that Brown was justified in his bloody exhibitions of character, because of the violence of pro-slavery men. Others suffered far more than he, and their brutal passions were never aroused into violence. And he was by no means the only one who heard threats of indiscriminate slaughter and extermination. For many months they were heard continually, and great coolness and forbearance were employed by Free State men everywhere, determined to act only on the defensive. The writer has many vivid recollections of those times, with his own painful experience; but he looked upon the persecutions as an offshoot of the accursed system he was laboring to put down, and looked forward with hope to the time when his efforts would be crowned with victory. It was this assurance of final success that nerved all, the humblest and highest, to press forward, and which has ultimated in giving freedom to the world.

John Brown, the professed Christian, should have taken lessons from his Exemplar, instead of showing such a thirst for blood. His character at Harper's Ferry, *after* he was wounded, while under arrest, his hopes blighted, and even while in the engine house in the treatment of prisoners, was in pleasing contrast with what he exhibited in Kansas, and seems almost irreconcilable with his disregard of human life at Pottawotomie.

CONFIRMATION.

I have been careful, throughout this series of articles, to make no statement of my own, that John Brown was directly connected with the Pottawotomie massacre; but I have arrayed such evidence as was in my possession, to prove this fact upon him. How successful I have been is left to others to decide. Allow me, reader, before I close, to add the additional facts which have come into my possession, as I hope to settle his question beyond further controversy.

A well-known gentleman of integrity, a prominent citizen of Lawrence, well known to me, since the spring of 1855, wrote me a private letter, of date Nov. 16, 1879, from which I make the following extract:

"Just before sunset, on the night of the massacre, I met old John Brown and his party, within a few miles of the Doyle settlement, on the Pottawotomie, and going in that direction. John Brown, Jr., and his company, were, at the time, in camp at Palmyra, this county. Old John Brown and his party left the camp early in the day, and did not return until the next day, when they came to the camp, then on 'Toywa creek near Jones'. * * I have never felt disposed to make the facts of that affair public."

Another gentleman of Lawrence wrote me. Nov. 23, 1879:

"I have been reading your articles on old John Brown. I am glad to see some one has the courage to write the truth about the Pottawotomie affair; but, good Lord, wont they go for you? I have often felt like telling what I know about it; but I was conscious those who were wholly ignorant of the facts, and were determined to remain so, would say I was telling that which was not true, hence I have remained silent."

Even John Speer, who has higgled over the most unimportant statements I have made in this series of articles, and who has always been recognized as the special champion of old John Brown, finding he could not sustain an *alibi*, and the proof of his guilt being so overwhelming, says, in an article which appeared in the Lawrence *Journal*, November 25, 1879:—

"I have taken great pains to get at the truth of the history of the 'Pottawotomie tragedy', visiting Pottawotomie and conversing with the men of Brown's time, with a view to facts. let them fall where they may. I find that the belief, confirmed by the traditions, go to the establishment of the fact that John Brown executed these men. That he ever mutilated their bodies, or did anything except what was necessary in their execution, I do not believe, nor does any man who knew John Brown."

John Speer is welcome to use the word "executed" in place of "*murdered*," as used by Robinson, of Paola, if he prefers. And as to the mutilation, I leave that with Phillips, in his story about the Camanches, and the sworn evidence of those who first discovered the bodies after the killing, as given under the head of "Details of the Massacre."

By private letters from Kansas, I learn that Hon. Jas. Hanway, whose cabin was photographed, and palmed off as old John Brown's, has made a statement through the press touching those murders; and while this article is in type for the press, I am in receipt of a letter from a prominent lawyer at Lawrence, stating:

"I am going this week to Osawotomie, to interview the man who gave Johnson Clark the facts; and expect to get his statement over his own signature. We shall soon have the whole history in detail. I think it a matter of importance that all the truth be known and published. I have been reading your articles with great interest."

THE CLINCHER.

Hidden away in a large book, the Kansas volume "United States Biographical Dictionary," and rarely seen by any person other than the few simpletons who paid twenty dollars for a copy of the work, with the additional pleasure of seeing their names in it, as "distinguished in history," is found the following statement, exhumed by JOHN HUTCHINGS, Esq., of Lawrence, Kan., and which he kindly gave to the public through the columns of the *Home Journal*, of Nov. 20, 1879, from which I quote at length. It is a statement made by Hon. Johnson Clark, of Miami county, Kan. Rather choice literature in this connection:

On May 24, 1855, William Sherman

called at the house of John T. Grant, a Free State man from New York, and there, in anger and in liquor, told the Grant family that they, (the pro-slavery men,) intended to drive out the Free State men from Pottawotomie Creek and othe parts of Kansas. This alarmed Grant, and he sent his son George to the camp of John Brown, who was at that time on Ottawa Creek, some twenty-five miles northwest. Upon arriving in camp, young Grant told John Brown the condition of things in his neighborhood, and the trouble anticipated if help was not had immediately. And here it is proper to state that news had come from Kansas City that Buford had organized and armed a large force of Georgia immigrants, and was about to march upon Kansas. The news had also arrived that Lawrence was in ashes, and that our Free State Governor, Robinson, was a prisoner in the hands of pro-slavery "border-ruffians," at Leavenworth. In brief, it was a time of terror so appalling that it was felt that the destiny of Kansas was trembling in the balance, and its fate about to be decided.

When old John Brown received this message from Pottawotomie, in addition to all other words of distress, a council was held in his camp. A party of eight was formed, headed and commanded by Brown himself. The names of the other members of this party were as follows: Frederick Brown, Owen Brown, Watson Brown, Oliver Brown, Henry Thompson, (Brown's son-in-law,) Mr. Wyner, and last the man who now lives in Kansas and gives me the particulars, and before whom I am now writing. This last-mentioned party, whom we will call Mr. T., took this party in his wagon and started from Ottawa Creek about two o'clock in the afternoon, arriving at the scene of the tragedy about midnight.

The first attack was upon a man by the name of Doyle and his two sons, they being parties that had threatened. They were immediately dispatched, and left lying in the woods near the cabin where they resided. They next visited the house of a man named Wilkinson, who was at the time a postmaster under Buchanan, and who lived about one-half mile from the Doyle residence, and Wilkinson was found dead the next morning. The party then proceeded to the premises of the Sherman brothers, which was across the creek, and about one mile distant. It was the intention to dispatch both these men, as they had been particularly active in the pro-slavery cause. Henry Sherman was out hunting cattle and had staid over night with a pro-slavery friend, but finding William, they called him out and left him dead in the middle of the creek, upon some rocks and gravel. They then wanted Mr. T to drive them to another place but it was now late at night, and he declined to take them any further.

Mr. T says that Brown's boys did most of the killing, by the advice and with the encouragement of old John Brown himself, and adds, further, that Brown himself, to nerve his party for the deeds about to be done, stepped in front of the first victim—the old man Doyle—and, drawing his revolver, shot him through the forehead. In conclusion, I will only add that this is the generally accepted version of the affair, in the vicinity of the tragedy, and that, notwithstanding historians have written to the contrary, I have no doubt but time will vindicate the correctness of this statement, which is from Mr. T., the only known witness living in the State. This Mr. T. is a quiet farmer, and now lives within a radius of a dozen miles of the dreadful scene he witnessed. This statement has been made to the writer of this, by Mr. T., a dozen times, and, in company with Judge James Hanway, I visited him at his house, where this is written, and, after hearing it read, he said: "It is correct." After a silence of a few moments he added: "I took no hand in the ki'ling, and did not approve of it, but Brown said: 'It must be done; it is better that a score of bad men should die than one man be driven from Kansas who came here to help make it a free State.'" JOHNSON CLARK.

Mr. Hutchings adds:

It will be seen by Mr. Clark's statement that the party that committed the Pottawotomie tragedy consisted of six members of the Brown family, and two others, one of whom at least was the "settler in the neighborhood."

CHANCE FOR CORRECTION.

These Reminiscences, as I contemplated when I commenced them, have awakened much interest in the Kansas

tors might see my statements, and correct any errors; as I did not flatter myself I could write of so many things, all occurring more than twenty years ago, relying almost wholly on memory, without being guilty of some mistakes. Indeed in my acceptance of Gov. Robinson's invitation to write of Old John Brown, I said:

"I shall endeavor to state nothing but facts, as seen from my own standpoint."

I did not propose to write from John Speer's standpoint, nor from that of my critics. Had I attempted it, probably my breadth of observation would have been far more limited. I might have seen some trifling matters quite differently; though from the former's exhibition of criticisms, which I shall notice further on, I think Truth would have suffered quite as much in his hands as in mine.

The Lawrence *Journal*, a Republican paper, published by T. D. Thacher, Esq., who has been identified with the Kansas press since 1857, kindly opened its columns, and is publishing the entire series, cheerfully giving space to correspondents to make corrections, for which I take this occasion to publicly thank the editor.

The Ottawa *Gazette*, a Democratic paper, published in Franklin county, in which the Pottowatomie murders occurred, edited by Joel K. Goodin, Esq., who was among the first settlers in Kansas, associated with us in all our early history, and who was the faithful secretary of the Territorial Executive Committee, and who certainly did more hard labor without recompense than any other man in Kansas, is also publishing the entire series. In a personal letter before me, he compliments the general accuracy of my statements, and says that my articles are giving general satisfaction.

Through these channels excellent opportunities have been offered to point out errors for emendation. Very few of such have come under my observation. These I will take occasion to correct

Gov. Robinson, at whose request these articles were written, in a communication press, and brought out a vast amount of facts, which, but for their publication, would have been lost to the world. Had I written, and deposited them in the archives of the Historical Society, the historian a few years later would have found the statements, and copied from them, and thus no opportunity would have been left for correction. I made it a condition of writing them that they should appear in three of the leading papers of Kansas, to the end that the acto the Lawrence *Journal*, of Nov 23d, says:

"*Dr. Brown's letters are so full of interest that I trust he will continue them till he has covered the whole field of Kansas history. I have seen no history that will compare in interest and accuracy with his letters; and a complete work from him would be invaluable.* Dr. Brown was no friend of mine, being estranged from me, for some cause I never fully understood, for eighteen months, so that we had no intercourse; yet the estrangement never prevented us acting together when the cause of Kansas called. The fact that Dr. Brown knew no friendship, but in the cause of free Kansas, makes him the fittest man to be the historian of Kansas."

CORRECTIONS.

While I have received a large number of letters, from prominent actors in those times, fully indorsing every material statement I have made, a few persons of an over critical turn of mind, and distressed at the loss of a "lesser god," have controverted several minor statements, predicated on information derived from others; and from these have attempted to weaken the force of my entire narration.

As before stated, I coveted criticism, to the end that truth only should be transmitted in these pages to those who come after us.

Instead of the principal facts being weakened by criticisms, every one has received confirmation; and the central figure has been presented in a more damaging attitude than I contemplated.

I stated, under the head of "History of a Revolver," that "the shooting of Sheriff Jones was the first blood actually drawn by Free State men in Kansas." To have been correct I should have said, as I desired to be understood, *it was the first aggressive act of violence by Free State men.* The killing of Henry Davis, by Lewis Kibby, Nov. 29, '54, was on the defensive; as was that of Malcom Clark, by Cole McCrea, at Leavenworth, April 30, '55.

I did not state that Charley Lenhart shot Sheriff Jones. I only gave the facts of the loan of the revolver, by Miss Gleason; the discharge, which she heard; the hasty return of Lenhart, with the revolver, minus one charge; and the deduction that it was Charley who did the shooting. By the statement of Capt. Swift, it appears that Lenhart did discharge the revolver, but not at Jones; that it was a Mr. Filer who inflicted the wound. The critic will turn to my account, and he will see that I did not err in fact, but in deduction.

As to the justice of applying the title of "Captain" to Lenhart, I have an original "order" in my possession, in Gen. Jas. H. Lane's hand writing, and signed by him, directed to "Captain Charles Lenhart," ordering him to "take such number of active young men as you shall deem necessary, and proceed with as little delay as possible to colonize Kickapoo." In due time I will place that document in the Historical Society of Kansas. Is not this sufficient authority for me to mention Charley with the title of Captain?

The rumor I gave that Lenhart was killed in a foolish attempt to rescue Capt. Brown, is also disproved. It seems he served his country during the first years of the rebellion, and died in Arkansas, with consumption, while yet in the service.

It is claimed that I was mistaken in the statement, that the Territorial Executive Committee was originally appointed at Big Springs, on the 5th of September, 1855; whereas it is represented they were appointed at Topeka fourteen days later. The question is not important; but I *think* I can demonstrate that my memory is correct in this case. Is it not strange that a new party was organized without any committee to represent it in the future? The committee, unless I am greatly mistaken, was appointed at Big Springs, and was organized by trickery, as I will show sometime, with Col. Lane, as Chairman. The Topeka Convention, on the 19th, was holden to consider the project of a State movement, and to prevent any collision of authority re-appointed the Big Springs' committee, with Lane as Chairman, and J. K. Goodin as Secretary. I wrote up the proceedings in detail, of the Big Springs convention, and published the same in the *Herald of Freedom.* The same matter was used in pamphlet form, two thousand copies of which were printed, and I have no doubt somebody has copies of them. If my memory serves me correctly, I was appointed with others, a committee to communicate the proceedings of the Big Springs convention to Gov. Shannon. Would I have been likely to have received this appointment if not a delegate?

I stated, as a fact, that I was invited by Gov. Robinson, who is President of the Historical Society of Kansas, to write these Reminiscences. The letter of invitation was published at the commencement of the series, and shows for itself, that *it was not done in his official capacity.* I am glad to write, however, that two copies of the entire work will be preserved by that body among its archives.

Again, my informant was somewhat mistaken in the time old John Brown left the camp of his son, going in the direction of Pottawotomie, and probably, as to the place and hour of his return. Human memory is treacherous. Possibly I did not report him accurately.

The charge that I have systemized the order of presenting my facts is puerile, and unworthy the head and heart of the critic making the objection. He who concedes so much reverence for his hero, and who, no doubt, indorsed the statement, credited to Ralph Waldo Emerson, that "The time will come when the gallows of old John Brown will be glorious like the cross of Christ," ought to tolerate a little honest skepticism in that direction.

A quotation is made from a letter it is said old John Brown wrote to Sanborn, to destroy the force of my facts, that the *Herald of Freedom* was in disrepute by Free State men. That paper was a foe to all forms of wrong doing, whether committed by pro-slavery men, or those acting in the Free State ranks. Jayhawkers, thieves and murderers, had reason to "despise it," and if John Brown associated with that class of "Free State men," he, no doubt, heard just such expressions as it is claimed he employed in regard to it. The position of the *Herald of Freedom* through all those times is one I can look back upon with pride, as I trust is the case with every other *honest* reader of it. Censure, from some persons, is the highest possible commendation.

Under the head of "John Brown in Lawrence," first paragraph, I said:

"I *think* there were seven *men* standing in the box. * * * Each man supported himself with a pole, *probably* six to eight feet in length, surmounted with a bayonet."

John Speer, the accurate critic and *very* truthful historian, represents that I said: "John Brown came with seven *sons*, armed with *pike* poles *ten* feet long."

Three additions in two lines! Now either John Speer misrepresented or was mistaken! Which? He had just read my statements, and, if disposed to play critic, should have been more accurate. Possibly there were but four *sons* and the father in the wagon. Does that render my statement, "I think there were seven *men* in the box," invalid? Twenty-four years lie between that event and the present, and, taking Speer's statement, I erred two-sevenths; while John Speer converts my "poles" "from six to eight feet in length," into "*pike* poles *ten* feet in length. And my "seven *men*" into seven *sons*," increasing the entire number to eight. Will some mathematician tell us how long the poles would have been, and what name they would have borne, had he waited twenty-four years before writing? And how many men would have been in the wagon, had he told the story after the same lapse of time?

Williams, riding behind, saw the party some distance back *sitting*, the old man with a rifle across his knees. Does this prove that they were not *standing* when they entered town? The poles were green ones, recently cut, and still covered with bark. Where they obtained them, or however numerous the denials, *I know* the poles were there, and the facts are just as I have stated.

I am charged with being a partisan of Gov. Robinson. From the 3d of July, 1856, to December 23d, 1857, Gov. R. and myself held no intercourse with each other. From that time to my leaving Kansas, nearly fifteen years ago, we only met a very few times, and then to advance the cause which took each of us to that Territory. I was never, in any sense, a partisan of Gov. Robinson; but let me do that gentleman and myself the justice to say, that while the breach between us was greatly widened by the action of the "professional letter writers," we came together, almost involuntarily, when we mutually felt that the freedom of Kansas was contingent on our harmonious action. From that time our personal animosities ceased, without explanation, and time, I trust, has satisfied each, that the other is in the main, at least as good as the average man, without regard to what the world may say in that direction.

Thus much for my reviewers. If any gentleman will write me, pointing out any other errors, it will give me pleasure to make the proper corrections when these pages shall be again put in type.

THE FLY ON THE LOCOMOTIVE.

We find running through recent accounts of John Brown's raid into Virginia, the very silly assertion that his attack, at Harper's Ferry, produced the Rebellion of the Southern States, and the emancipation of the slaves in consequence. This assertion is of a similar character with that of the eastern press in representing the Pottawotomie massacre as the outgrowth of the killing of Frederick Brown, which antedated the killing by more than three months.

The South had threatened the nullification of United States laws, as early as 1832-33, and a general conspiracy for secession was set on foot; but the whole movement was suppressed by the master mind of Jackson. Through all the years that followed to 1861, the critical observer saw that we were standing on the verge of a smouldering volcano, ready to burst forth at any time. Calhoun and associate conspirators were ever active in furtherance of their desires, while Benton, Clay and Webster were equally energetic to thwart their purposes.

Southern success in securing the admission of Texas; the passage of the compromise measures of 1850; and the acquisition of newly acquired territory, suspended their action for a time. They lost control of the House of Representatives, in 1856; and the admission of Kansas into the Union in 1861, destroyed their last hope of controlling either branch of Congress; for this, with the admission of Minnesota, gave the North a heavy preponderance in that body, which they knew they could never regain.

The united South had hoped to make Kansas a slave State. They knew it was the key which would decide the fate of Nebraska, Colorado, New Mexico, Nevada, Arizona, Montana, Utah, etc. Failing to secure their wishes in this respect; and, to crown the causes for distress, in a square issue between the North and South, a northern President was elected. They decided to submit the question to the arbitrament of war, hoping through it if they regained nothing, they would prevent what they deemed further aggressions.

Possibly the invasion of Virginia, under the circumstances, may have been employed by southern demagogues as an instrumentality to further inflame the southern heart; but this was never their pretext in a single State paper. They complained of the disregard of solemn covenants, on the part of the North; of continued interference, both in Congress and out of it, with their peculiar institutions; they said that legislation had prohibited slavery in the District of Columbia, in violation of good faith; that the fugitive slave law was a dead letter on the statute books; that their rights were everywhere disregarded.

The faithful historian has at all times stated the fact, that the contest between freedom and slavery in Kansas, inaugurated the rebellion, and ultimated in the freedom of a continent. The other allegation is the product of such minds as

James Redpath and his congeries of Northern disunionists, who, like the fly on the driving wheel of a locomotive pompously exclaimed, "Look and see what a vast train I am moving!"

HERO WORSHIP.

"Woe to that man who does not reverence the gods we set up." It is no less true to-day than in the days of Nebuchadnezzar. The fiery furnace of public opinion is ever burning, and ever ready to consume those who will not obey the popular mandate. "Away with him, crucify him," is heard on every hand, through every age, directed against all bold enough to have and express an honest thought.

When the Egyptian god Serapis was destroyed, in the year 385, by the order of Theodosius, at the instance of the Christian Bishop of Alexandria, and the remaining 350,000 volumes of the great Alexandrian library was burned, with the temple, the people looking on were horrified beyond expression. They had been taught that Serapis caused the Nile to overflow and fertilize the country. They thought, following this indignity to their god, and the desecration of his temple, the great river would cease to give its annual tribute to the soil; that productive harvests would cease; and starvation follow. No terms were sufficiently expressive with which to denounce the authors of their sorrow. They were sincere in their denunciations, and really believed the threats of their priests would be executed to the letter.

The seasons rolled on; the waters came down from the mountains at their accustomed time, and brought the usual fertilizing productions; the valley of the Nile was clothed with beauty and verdure. Though Serapis was dead the golden harvests were as luxuriant as ever. The people were fed. Peace and prosperity reigned. Soon the deluded devotee saw that his imagined deity had not the power to interrupt the great processes of Nature, and his name was no longer revered.

It is so with regard to all heroes. They are the idols of the age in which they live, and are worshipped as such. Statues are erected to their memory when dead. Costly monuments adorn their resting places; and lying epitaphs perpetuate the popular applause. Another generation goes by. Cool reflection takes the place of the frenzied hour; histories are ransacked; the truth is learned: the hero of yesterday is forgotten to day; and, like Marat in French history, his bones are removed from their resting place by the side of kings; his portraits are torn down and trampled upon; his mausoleum is demolished; and fragments of his costly monument are all that remain of him whom a "grateful nation" so highly idolized as to vote a pension for life to his *concubine*.

CONCLUSION.

I knew full well that the task I attempted—to correct the false in history—was an unpopular one. I was aware, before a single line was written, that popular prejudice had enshrined a hero, and, as in classic story, his devotees were "filling the air with hideous shrieks and shouts, and crying aloud, 'Great is Bacchus!'" Occupying too humble a position to feel the shock of their blows, and too strong in the rectitude of my intentions to be diverted from my purpose; fully conscious of my inability to do justice to what I had undertaken, I have continued TO THE END, content to leave to the conscientious and unprejudiced reader, and to future times, the rendition of their verdict. Whether I have contributed any what of facts to aid in placing in his true position, in American history, the Guerilla Chieftain and Visionary Enthusiast, the 'gallant and intrepid' OLD JOHN BROWN?

As the earth from a fiery beginning, with convulsions of a most gigantic character; the incessant roar of contending elements; upheavals and depressions; volcanic eruptions and rivers of molten rock, and showers of scoriæ and ashes; geysers, everywhere sending up floods of boiling water, dissolving into vapor, and descending in torrents, falling on heated rock to again ascend as steam, forming clouds which obscured for ages sun and stars; lightnings ever flashing along the sky, with crash on crash of deafening thunders; earthquakes rending the globe, and upheaving mountains and depressing valleys; all nature everywhere discordant; hurricanes and cyclones ever active; —thence change following change in gradual succession from age to age, until the present delightful era, when the earth is clothed with beauty, adorned with verdure, and animal life fills up the waste places, and man appears to crown the whole with wisdom and joy;—so we have seen Kansas, torn and convulsed by contending factions; neighbor warring with neighbor; Anarchy and Discord sweeping over the land, amid pillaged homes, burning dwellings, scattered families, death and mutilation, grim-visaged famine, desolating pestilence, conflagrations, and all the multitudinous ills that humanity is subject to;—thence tranquility, and order, and beaming peace; labor largely rewarded, and prosperity attendant upon every enterprise; commerce spreading her whitened sales; the school room showering intelligence upon her youth; joyous homes everywhere springing up, while Contentment is smiling at every door, as we find it to-day; and, bending in silent but humble adoration, before that Wisdom which crowns all with peace and happiness, we bid the reader, for the present, a cheerful FAREWELL!

THE END.

APPENDIX.

The admirers of old John Brown must desire the possession of every important fact that throws light upon his history While the preceeding sketches were passing through the Kansas press a vast amount of new information, heretofore concealed in the breasts of interested partisan friends, have come to light. Such as has fallen under the observation of the writer, I propose to add in this Appendix, and shall conclude with a Review, from Hon. Eli Thayer, of Massachusetts, which will only appear in the pamphlet.

VALUABLE CORRESPONDENCE.

WORCESTER, Mass., Dec. 10, 1879.

DR. G. W. BROWN:—I have received, and read with the greatest interest, your "Reminiscences of old John Brown." I earnestly hope you will continue these papers until they embrace all the important facts of the early Kansas history.

I inclose herewith a letter which I received last summer from Hon. Geo. A. Crawford, of Fort Scott, Kansas, in relation to John Brown's Pottawotomie Massacre, and his raid into Missouri, which I think may be of use to you, and which I would like to have preserved in the Kansas Historical Society.

I am confident that Mr. Crawford will not object to its publication. Mr. C., in advising John Brown to leave the Territory, in my opinion, gave expression to the general desire of the men who made Kansas a Free State. *   *   *

Thanking you sincerely for the great work you are doing for the truth of history, I remain, very truly yours,

ELI THAYER.

FORT SCOTT, Kan., Aug. 4, 1879.

HON. ELI THAYER, Worcester, Mass.

MY DEAR SIR:—Yours of the 28th ult. received asking for facts in my possession in regard to John Brown's participation in what is known as the Pottawotomie massacre, and the raid into Missouri.

In reply I would state that I was in John Brown's camp, at the Trading Post, in Linn county, Kansas, early in January, 1859, and had conversations with him in regard to both transactions.

As to the "Massacre" he said he would not say that he was *not* engaged in it, but he *would* say that he advised it, and justified it, and was willing to take a full share of the responsibility of it. He said that the death of those pro-slavery men had been determined upon, at a meeting of free state settlers the day before; that he was present at that meeting, and, I think, presided, and that the executioners were then and there appointed. He said he would not say that he was one of them, but he would say that if it was wrong he was as much to blame as any.

He gave as a reason for the deed that *the men were carriers of news to the Missourians,* that they kept a "grape-vine telegraph" with Missourians, and were endangering the settlements, by bringing in the invaders. He said it became necessary to make an example, and so strike terror, and put an end to that sort of thing.

As to the raid into Missouri—it was made on the 20th Dec. 1858, four days after the raid into Fort Scott. It was led by Capt. Brown in person. Capt. Montgomery refused to go along—protested, as I have understood, against it,—but came to the aid of the Kansas settlers when retaliatory raids were afterwards expected. The Captain's Company marched down the Little Osage River, in the north part of this county, and about 12 miles from here, and proceeded into Vernon Co., Mo., a distance of three or four miles.

The Missouri *Democrat*, of Dec. 30th, 1858, gave the Missouri statement of the losses. I presume it is correct. Files of other papers of the period would show. It states that they "murdered" David Crews, (or Cruise,) "kidnapped a negro woman," took wagon, horses &c., and robbed Mr. Martin and family of a fine mule; took from the estate of James Lawrence, in possession of his son-in-law Henry Hicklin, five negroes, 2 horses, 1 yoke of cattle, an ox-wagon, a double barrel shot gun, saddle and clothing. From Isaac B. LaRue, five negroes, six horses, 1 yoke of cattle, clothing—and took prisoners whom they released.

In the conversation to which I have alluded, Captain Brown said he had sent the slaves on to their freedom; that they had earned the property of their masters; and that his young men were entitled to forage to the extent of their subsistence. He denied the current rumor that the slaves had been taken away by violence and against their will.

As to the killing of Cruise, he said that he had given strict orders for the careful use of the guns; and that there should be no firing unless resistance was offered. He had divided his men into two squads, one on each side of the stream. In the house of Cruise one of his quick-blooded young men, supposing that Cruise was about to draw a weapon, had fired, killing him instantly. I inferred that the Captain was not present. He claimed to have reprimanded the young man for his haste.

Cruise was a good citizen—a plain unoffending farmer. It was reported that he had no weapons on his person. The killing of him was an unjustifiable outrage, and it subjected our settlements to great danger from retaliatory measures.

I protested to the Captain against this violence. We were settlers, he was not. He could strike a blow and leave. The retaliatory blow would fall on us. Being a free-state man, I myself, was held personally responsible by pro-slavery ruffians in Ft. Scott, for the acts of Capt. Brown.

One of these ruffians, Brockett, when they gave me notice to leave the town said: " When a snake bites me I don't go hunting for that particular snake. I kill the first snake I come to."

I called Capt. Brown's attention to the facts that we were at peace with Missouri; that our Legislature was then in the hands of Free-State men, to make the laws; that even in our disturbed counties of Bourbon and Linn we were in a majority, and had elected the officers both to make and execute the laws; that without peace we could have no immigration; that no southern immigration was coming; that agitation, such as his, was only keeping our northern friends away, &c.

The old man replied that it was no pleasure to him—an old man—to be living in the saddle, away from home and family, and exposing his life; and if the free-state men of Kansas felt that they no longer needed him he would be glad to go.

He seemed very erratic—at war with all our accustomed ideas on the slavery question—but very earnest.

I think the conversation made an impression on him, for he soon after went to his self-sacrifice at Harper's Ferry.

Yours,   Geo. A. Crawford.

THE POTAWATOMIE TRAGEDY—COL. BLOOD'S RECOLLECTION.

Rockford, Ill., Nov. 19, 1879.

Jas. Blood, Esq.

My Dear Sir:—Yours of the 16th is at hand, and I hasten to reply.

Twenty years ago I made a statement of the Potawatomie massacre in the *Herald of Freedom*. After writing it, but before passing to the compositors, I chanced to meet a gentleman to whom I alluded in my recent statement. He suggested several corrections, which were made in his presence, and re-read to him;

when he said the statement, as amended, was correct, and he would make affidavit to it, if the truth should ever be called in question. He further made the additional statements at the time which I have added. I asked leave to refer to him then. He declined, saying he did not wish to be mixed up in the matter, but sometime he would take pleasure in stating all his knowledge on the subject.

I did think of sending him the statement for his indorsement before publishing at this time; but was so sure that my memory served me correctly, and had such confidence in his statement, that, in the hurry, with the length of time that must intervene between writing and publication, I gave it to the printers without consultation with him.

In all cases where possible I have given the names of living witnesses and wish I could do so in every instance.

I think you will excuse me for not giving at present the name you request, but I will take great pleasure in correcting, at the close of the series of articles, which is now near at hand, *any errors* which I have been led into by misstatements of others, or defective memory, as it is my desire that the truth, and the truth only, be stated in the premises.

The whole matter is being stereotyped as we advance, and it is expected that the edition, in pamphlet or book form, will be large; hence I ask it as a favor to the public and, to another generation, for whom I principally write, that every error be corrected in the same volume in which the original statement is made.

I am satisfied that you are in possession of valuable facts in the matter. I have always known you as a gentleman of the strictest truth; your opportunities of observation, through all these times, were large; neither of us have anything to gain by concealment, or to lose by the fullest exposure. Those who come after us have a right to be fully informed of the times in which we lived; therefore I again ask you to give me a full and frank statement of the facts, without any reflections on anybody, and it shall have as wide circulation as the original statement.

Thanking you for your kindness in writing me, and wishing that any and all other persons having knowledge on this subject would be equally frank, and write me direct, to the end that I may, in my closing articles, make the proper corrections, I am, with pleasant old-time memories, Very truly yours,

G. W. BROWN.

COLONEL BLOOD'S REPLY.

LAWRENCE, Kan., Nov. 29. 1879.

G. W. BROWN, M. D., ROCKFORD, Ill.—*Dear Sir:* Yours of the 19th inst., was duly received, but I have hesitated to comply with your request to write for publication a statement of what I know about the "Potawatomie massacre," in 1856. I was not "an eye witness," but have concluded to make a statement of incidents that came within my observation, as I recollect them.

In the spring of 1856, I went east on business, leaving my family in Lawrence. I was in New Hampshire, when I learned that the border ruffians were gathering, under ruffianly federal officers, to destroy Lawrence. I immediately started for home, arriving at Kansas City, I think, on the 21st day of May, 1856. I could find no way of getting to Lawrence, direct, but hired a close hack to take me, with two or three friends (one of them was J. F. Bliss, now residing at Oskaloosa,) to Ossawatomie. We instructed the driver to say to any one who might halt us, that he was taking some men to Pleasant Hill, Missouri. We drove south through Westport, and the parties halting us appeared to be satisfied with the reply of the driver. We stayed that night at a farm house in Missouri, a short distance south of Westport. The next day, the 22nd, we took dinner with Baptiste Peoria, where Paola now stands, and arrived at Osawatomie in the afternoon. From there we sent the hack back to Kansas City.

The next morning I bought a horse of O. C. Brown—who will be remembered by the old settlers as the original Osawatomie Brown. After having the horse shod, I started in the afternoon of the 23rd of May, from Osawatomie for Lawrence, by way of Ottawa Jones' and Palmyra.

I was informed while at Osawatomie that the active pro-slavery men of that part of the Territory had gone to Lecompton to join the border ruffians in their attack upon Lawrence, and that most of the Free State men had gone, under the lead of Capt. John Brown, Jr., to aid in the defence of Lawrence,

It was nearly sun-down that afternoon when, between Potawatomie Creek and Middle Creek, and but a few miles from the Doyle settlement, I saw a party of men coming from the west and going toward Potawatomie Creek. As we approached each other I could see the gleam of the sun's rays reflected from the moving gun-barrels of the party, in a wagon. When within perhaps 100 yards they stopped, and a man rose up in the wagon and cried, halt! I immediately recognized old John Brown, and stated who I was, calling him by name. I was then allowed to approach the party. There were in the wagon John Brown, and, to the best of my recollection, four of his sons, his son-in-law, and a man driving the team, whom I did not know, making seven in the wagon. There was also a man on horseback, I think his name was Wymer, or Winer.

The party all appeared to be fully armed with rifles, revolvers, knives or swords. I think some of them at least had a peculiar instrument, something like a Scotch claymore, or a short, very heavy broadsword. John Brown had presented me with one of the same kind, while at Lawrence, during the Wakarusa war, in the fall of 1855.

I talked with the old man for some time. I believe he was the only one of the party who spoke. He stated that they had left Capt. John Brown Jr., with the Potawatomie company, in camp near Palmyra. He informed me that Lawrence had been sacked and burned, and that a number of leading Free State men had been taken prisoners. He seemed very indignant that there had been no resistance; that Lawrence was not defended; and denounced the members of the committee and leading Free State men as cowards, or worse. His manner was wild and frenzied, and the whole party watched with excited eagerness every word and motion of the old man. Finally, as I left them, he requested me not to mention the fact that I had met them, as they were on a *secret expedition*, and did not want any one to know that they were in that neighborhood.

I came on, and when I arrived at Middle Creek it was dark,—so dark that immediately after crossing the creek I lost the road, and after riding some time returned to the crossing, where I found the road and arrived at Jones' late in the night.

The next morning, the 24th, I again started for Lawrence. When I arrived at Palmyra, I found the Potawatomie company, with one or two other companies of Free State men, and there learned that Capt. John Brown, Jr., had gone to Lawrence to learn the condition of things there.

I rode on toward Lawrence, and met Capt. Brown, Jr., south of Wakarusa. From him I obtained the first reliable information as to what had taken place at Lawrence. He appeared to be in good spirits and perfectly rational.

When a day or two later we heard of the massacre of the Doyles, Wilkinson, and Sherman, on the Potawatomie, on the night of the 23d, I could have no doubt as to who committed the deed. I could not resist the conviction that it was done with those Scotch claymores. I remembered the wild frenzied look and appearance of old John Brown and his party, when I met them near the Potawatomie settlement, on that evening, and only a few hours before those men were killed.

I believe the Free State men here regarded this horrible tragedy with more sincere and sorrowful regret than any other incident of our struggle. It was regarded as terribly damaging to the Free State party and cause. No sufficient justification or defence could be made.

I sincerely believed that it was the work of insane men. Their halting at that distance a solitary traveler, who was apparently unarmed, and upon the open prairie where they could see for miles around, seemed to me evidence of insanity. Certainly that number of so well-armed men could not fear an assault and capture, or that they were in any immediate danger. I noticed that while we were in conversation the boys watched every look and gesture of the old man—keeping their guns in their hands ready for instant action.

A short time after the Potawatomie massacre I had a conversation with George Partridge, an old acquaintance and friend of mine from Wisconsin, who was then a settler on the Potawatomie. He was a strong anti-slavery man, and was killed later that summer in the fight at Osawatomie.

Mr. Partridge informed me that he was

a member of Capt. John Brown, Jr's. company, and was with them on their expedition to Palmyra, in May. He stated that old John Brown became frenzied at the condition of affairs in the Territory, and the refusal or failure of Free State men to fight; that the old man left the company, on the 23rd, with six or seven others, and against the remonstrance of his son, Capt. John Brown, Jr.; that when, on the afternoon and evening of the 24th, while in camp at Ottawa Jones',news was received of the massacre, Captain Brown, Jr., became insane, and was taken home the next day a maniac.

Mr. Partridge also stated that the only provocation the Doyles had given; as far as he knew, was, that *at the spring election, a short time before, Doyle expressed his dislike for negroes and abolitionists, and that Brown expressed his dislike of pro slavery men. He said that denunciations and threats were made on both sides.* *

In the foregoing I have stated the incidents as I recollect them. Mr. Partridge had no doubt that the killing was done by old John Brown and his party, and sincerely regretted the affair.

I believe that when we heard here of the Potawatomie massacre Col. Samuel Walker was sent down there by the committee (of which Gen. Babcock was chairman,) to learn all the facts in relation to the matter. Perhaps Colonel Walker or Gen. Babcock could furnish some information on the subject.

Respectfully,   J. BLOOD.

* Of all the fifteen or over different motives given for this terrible massacre, including that by Capt. Brown himself, to Gov. Crawford, this, by Mr. Partridge, to Col. Blood, seems the most plausible.—BROWN.

STATEMENT OF THE GRANTS.

Geo. W. Grant, a son of John T. Grant, mentioned by Johnson Clark, in an article headed "CLINCHER," made a statement to the Lawrence *Journal* a few weeks ago, the greater substance of which is given below, from that paper, as follows:

"We were near neighbors of the Shermans, of the Doyles, and Wilkinson.

"When the news came that the Border Ruffians were about to attack Lawrence, the Free State men of Potawatomie Creek raised a company to go to the rescue. It was under command of Capt. John Brown, Jr. I was a member of the company. We started for Lawrence, but on the way there a messenger reached us saying it was too late; that the town was already sacked. While lying in camp the company was drawn up one day, and old John Brown called for volunteers, saying: "*How many men will volunteer to go with me and obey my orders?*" When he called for volunteers John Brown, Jr., said: "Father, I object to any of the men leaving. We are getting up near the enemy and may need them." After the number had volunteered John Brown, Jr., said, "Father, be careful and commit no rash act." The volunteers were Fred, Owen, Salmon and Oliver Brown, Thompson, John Brown's son-in-law, Mr. Winer, and Mr. Townsley, with his team. After they had volunteered they went into camp by themselves, and *ground up their sabres.* They were armed with short swords or sabres.

"When we were at Ottawa Jones', the Brown party came in during the night. The next morning I saw one of Dutch Henry's horses, which they had brought in. It was a gray horse, with mane and tail sheared. We had heard of the killing on Pottawatomie Creek, at Palmyra, and had returned.

"The effect of the news of the massacre on John Brown, Jr., was very marked. He showed great agitation, and gave up the command of the company to H. H. Williams."

[Then follows a long account of the provocation for the massacre. As we have at least fifteen different reasons given, one by Capt. Brown himself to Gov. Crawford, we will not tax the reader with any additional ones.]

"They were apparently killed by a thrust with the short sword, and by cuts over the head with the sabre, except Doyle, who was shot in the forehead, and also stabbed. There was no idea at that time that the bodies had been purposely mutilated. The wounds in the hands had apparently been made either in attempting to ward off blows, or in grasping the blades of the short swords.

Mrs. Wilkinson's description of the leader pointed out Brown as present at the killing. She mentioned his being an old man, and his wearing a black stock about his neck, which Brown habitually wore. *Nobody on the creek doubted that John Brown was the leader of the party.* As to the killing, it was the current story that Brown shot Doyle, but personally did nothing more, and that the cutting and stabbing was done by other members of the party.

The effect of this massacre on the inhabitants of the creek, was to greatly alarm both parties. The pro-slavery settlers almost entirely left at once and the Free State people were constantly fearful of vengeance. As a matter of fact, there was no more killing on either side in that neighborhood. Dutch Henry—Henry Sherman, was killed in the spring of 1857, but politics had nothing to do with it."

To this statement, in the *Journal* of Dec. 11th, 1879, is affixed the signatures of Geo. W. & H. C. Grant.

The following appeared as an editorial in the Lawrence, Kan. *Standard*, of Dec. 11th, 1879:

"WERE THEY MUTILATED?"

Mr. Townsley, in his statement about the Pottawatomie massacre, says that the bodies of the Doyles were not mutilated, or at least not to his knowledge Mr. Ely Moore, who is employed in the Standard office, says that he arrived at the scene of the murder before the bodies were cold, that the ears and noses of old man Doyle and one of his sons were cut off, and that old man Doyle had a great gash down the side of his face, cut apparently with a sword or sabre. John Brown's pistol ball entered just over the eye.

MR. TOWNSLEY'S STATEMENT.

The statement of Mr. Townsley, given below, was procured by John Hutchings, Esq., of Lawrence, Kansas, referred to at the close of my article headed "Confirmation." In answer to the question, "Who is Mr. Townsley?" the Lawrence, Kan., *Journal* says:

James Townsley, whose statement in regard to the Potawatomie affair we publish this morning, was one of the first settlers in Anderson county. In Johnson's history of that county we notice that he was one of the Commissioners who located its first county seat, at a place called Shannon, March 1, 1856. At that place all the county business was transacted until April 5, 1856. He was also one of the Commissioners who located in the same month the first road in the county, running from Shermanville [Dutch Henry's Crossing] through the county seat to Hampden and Cofachique. Most, if not all of these places now exist only in history, and it is said that only a few persons in the county can point out the place even where the first county seat stood. Mr. Townsley's history, however, is not likely to be so ephemeral. The closeness of his relation to the hero of Harper's Ferry in one of the most striking if not important acts of his life, will be likely to secure for his name a remembrance not soon to be extinguished.

I am a native of Hartford county, state of Maryland, and was born August 29, 1815. I enlisted in company I, Capt. Benjamin L. Bell, Second United States dragoons, and served five years in the war waged against the Seminole and Creek Indians, a part of the time under the command of Gen. Taylor, and was discharged in August, 1844, at Fort Washita, Indian territory. I am a painter by trade, and followed that business in Fallston, in my native county, until October 20, 1855, when I emigrated to Kansas with my family, and settled in Anderson county, on the Potawatomie creek, about one mile west of Greeley. I joined the Potawatomie rifle company at its re-organization in May, 1856, at which time John Brown, Jr., was elected captain. On the 21st of the same month information was received that the Georgians were marching on Lawrence, threatning its destruction. The company was immediately called together, and about 4 o'clock p. m. we started on a forced march to aid in its defense. About two miles south of Middle Creek we were joined by the Osawatomie company, under Capt. Dayton, and proceeded to Mount Vernon, where we waited about two hours, until the moon rose. We then marched all night, camping the next morning, the 22d, for breakfast, near Ottawa Jones'. Before we arrived at this point news had been received that Lawrence had been destroyed, and a question was raised whether we should return or go on. During the forenoon, however, we proceeded up Ottawa creek to within about five miles of Palmyra, and went into camp near the residence of Captain Shore. Here we remained undecided over night. About noon the next day, the 23d, old John Brown came to me and said he had just received information that trouble was expected on the Potawatomie, and wanted to know if I would take my team and take him and his boys back so that they could keep watch of what was going on. I told him I would do so. The party consisting of old John Brown, Frederick Brown, Owen Brown, Watson Brown, Oliver Brown, Henry Thompson [John Brown's son-in-law,] and Mr. Winer, were soon ready for the trip, and we started, as near as I can remember, about 2 o'clock p. m. All of the party, except Mr. Winer, who rode a pony, rode with me in my wagon. When within two or three miles of the Potawatomie creek, we turned off the main road to the right, drove down to to the edge of the timber between two deep ravines, and camped about one mile above Dutch Henry's crossing.

After my team was fed and the party had taken supper, John Brown told me for the first time what he proposed to do. He said he wanted me to pilot the company up to the forks of the creek, some five or six miles above, into the neighborhood where I lived, and show them where all the pro-slavery men resided; that *he proposed to sweep the creek as he came down of all the pro-slavery men living on it.* I positively refused to do it. He insisted upon it, but when he found that I would not go he decided to postpone the expedition until the following night. I then wanted to take my team and go home, but he would not let me do so, and said I should remain with them. We remained in camp that night and all day the next day. Sometime after dark we were ordered to march.

We started, the whole company, in a northerly direction, crossing Mosquito creek above the residence of the Doyles. Soon after crossing the creek some one of the party knocked at the door of a cabin, but received no reply—I have forgotten whose cabin it was, if I knew at the time. The next place we came to was the residence of the Doyles. John Brown, three of his sons and son-in-law went to the door, leaving Frederick Brown, Winer, and myself a short distance from the house. About this time a large dog attacked us. Frederick Brown struck the dog a blow with his short two-edged sword, after which I dealt him a blow with my sabre, and heard no more of him. The old man Doyle and two sons were called out and marched some distance from the house toward Dutch Henry's in the road, where a halt was made. *Old John Brown drew his revolver and shot the old man Doyle in the forehead*, and Brown's two youngest sons immediately fell upon the younger Doyles with their short two-edged swords.

One of the young Doyles was stricken down in an instant, but the other attempted to escape, and was pursued a short distance by his assailant and cut down. The company then proceeded down Mosquito creek to the house of Allen Wilkinson. Here the old man Brown, three of his sons, and son-in-law, as at the Doyle residence, went to the door and ordered Wilkinson to come out, leaving Frederick Brown, Winer and myself standing in the road east of the house. Wilkinson was taken and marched some distance south of his house and slain in the road, with a short sword, by one of the younger Browns. After he was killed his body was dragged out to one side and left.

We then crossed the Potawatomie and came to the house of Henry Sherman, generally known as Dutch Henry. Here John Brown and the party, excepting Frederick Brown, Winer, and myself, who were left outside a short distance from the door, went into the house and brought out one or two persons talked with them some, and then took them in again. They afterward brought out William Sherman, Dutch Henry's brother, marched him down into the Potawatomie creek, where he was slain with swords by Brown's two youngest sons, and left lying in the creek.

It was the expressed intention of Brown to execute Dutch Henry also, but he was not found at home. He also hoped to find George Wilson, Probate Judge of Anderson County, there, and intended, if he did, to kill him too. Wilson had been notifying Free State men to leave the territory. I had received such a notice from him myself.

I desire to say here that it is not true that there was any intentional mutilation of the bodies after they were killed. They were slain as quickly as possible and left, and whatever gashes they received were inflicted in the process of cutting them down with swords. I understand that the killing was done with these swords so as to avoid alarming the neighborhood by the discharge of firearms.

I desire also to say that I did not then approve of the killing of those men, but *Brown said it must be done, for the protection of the Free State settlers;* that it was better that a score of bad men should die than that one man who came here to make Kansas a free state should be driven out.

Brown wanted me to pilot the party into the neighborhood where I lived, and point out all the pro-slavery men in it, whom he proposed to put to death. I positively refused to do it, and on account of my refusal I remained in camp all of the night upon which the first attack was to be made, and the next day. I told him I was willing to go with him to Lecompton and attack the leaders, or fight the enemy in open field anywhere, but I did not want to engage in killing these men. That night and the acts then perpetrated are vividly fixed in my memory, and I have thought of them many times since.

I then thought that the transaction was terrible, and have mentioned it to but few persons since. In after time, however, I became satisfied that it resulted in good to the Free State cause, and was especially beneficial to the Free State settlers on Potawatomie creek. The pro-slavery men were dreadfully terrified, and large numbers of them soon left the territory. It was afterward said that one Free State man could scare a company of them. I always understood that Geo. W. Grant came to our camp on Ottawa creek, near Capt. Shore's, with a message from his father, John T. Grant, to John Brown, asking for protection from threatened assaults of the Shermans and other pro-slavery ruffians. But I did not know Geo. W. Grant at the time, and do not remember of seeing him. I frequently heard the circumstance mentioned as a fact. After the killing of William Sherman, some time after midnight, we all went back to camp, about one mile distant, where we had left my team and other things. We remained in camp until after noon of the following day, and then started to join the Potawatomie company under John Brown, Jr. When we reached Ottawa Jones' about midnight, we found them in camp at that place.

The next morning the company was called together just after breakfast, and John Brown, Jr., announced his resignation, and requested the company to elect another captain in his place. The name of H. H. Williams, now of Osawatomie, and my own were presented and a vote taken which resulted in the election of Williams. The company then broke camp and started for home. After crossing Middle Creek at Mount Vernon, John Brown, with the rest of the party who accompanied him on the Potawatomic expedition, fell back from the balance of the company and struck off to the left of the main Potawatomie road, in the direction of the cabins of John Brown, Jr., and Jason Brown. That night we staid at the cabin of the former, keeping up a guard all night. The next night we went to Jason Brown's, about one mile and a half away. Here we remained several days, all the time on the watch. While we remained here August Bundy, and I think Benjamin L. Cochran, joined us. After several days, as I now remember, a young man by the name of Carpenter came to us from Prairie City and gave the information that Capt. Pate was in the vicinity in search of Brown. That evening we all took horses and started for Prairie City, where we arrived next morning about daylight and camped in the timber on Ottawa creek, near Capt. Shore's. While John Brown was cooking breakfast for the company, James Redpath came into our camp and had some conversation with Capt. Brown.

I saw Redpath again after the battle of Black Jack, near Blue Mound, and I desire to say in this connection, that I never told Redpath at any time that John Brown was not present at the Pottawotomie tragedy. His statement, which was read to me, to the effect that "two squatters, who aided in the execution," gave him such information, is totally false, so far as I am concerned. As Winer and myself were the only settlers in the neighborhood not members of Brown's family who were present at the tragedy, I can only conclude he referred to us. In the afternoon, after we camped in the woods near Capt. Shore's, we moved up to Prairie City. We picketed out our horses and laid down not over a hundred yards from the store. About the middle of the afternoon six of Pate's men came riding into town, four of whom we captured and held as prisoners. During the afternoon Capt. Shore raised a company of about thirty men, and in the evening we started in pursuit of Pate. The next morning before daylight we obtained information that he was camped at Black Jack point, and we moved forward with about twenty-four men to attack him. When within a mile of Pate's forces we all dismounted, left seven men in charge of the horses, and, with seventeen men, made the attack. In about fifteen minutes we drove them into the ravine. The fight continued about three hours when

Pate surrendered. About the time we got the captured arms loaded into the wagons ready to move, Maj. Abbott's company came up and we all marched back to Prairie City with the prisoners. Here we remained until Col. Sumner released them.

At this time I left John Brown, and in company with Charley Lenhart and many other Lawrence parties, camped in the timber near Ottawa Jones'.

I make this statement at the urgent request of my friends and neighbors, Judge James Hanway and Hon. Johnson Clarke, who have been present during all the time occupied in writing it out, and in whose hearing it has been several times read before signing.

JAMES TOWNSLEY.

LANE, Kan., Dec. 6, 1879.

CONFIRMATORY LETTER FROM COL. WALKER.

LAWRENCE, Kan., Dec. 21, 1879.

DR. G. W. BROWN—Dear Sir:—I have just read your article in your John Brown series, entitled "Another Invasion." You are correct in your statement that Maj. Abbott was in command on the day you mention. He was appointed officer of the day on the 13th, and was not relieved on Sunday morning, the 14th, as Gen. Lane was away, and no one was named to succeed him. When news came in on Sunday that the enemy was moving on Lawrence, Maj. Abbott asked me what he should do. I told him to keep on his sash, and do the best he could. He ordered me to get what mounted men I could, and go to Franklin, and reconnoitre in that direction and gain such intelligence as I could of the enemy's movements. All the mounted men I could find in the city numbered only ten. When we started out I saw your sister, Mrs. Mandell, with a rifle in her hands.

John Brown had no command of any kind on that day. The men with me were the first to exchange shots with the invaders. Coming back we met the Stubbs, under Capt. Cracklin, marching in the direction from which we came. The next morning John Brown was gone —no one knew where.

Gov. Geary, in making terms with the invading forces, consented to let that portion of them which belonged North, pass through the city, and cross the river on the ferry. When Maj. Abbott heard of it he came to me, and said that it would never do to let the d—d skunks pass through the city in triumph. He and I mounted our horses and rode to Gov. Geary's quarters, on the hill, and told him we would never consent to allow an armed force to pass through the city—if no one else would fire on them we would, and thus would bring on a collision. The Governor consulted with Col. Cooke, and the latter labored to convince us that the Governor was right. But we refused to yield. The Governor finally issued an order, which was executed by an orderly, directing the party to pass up the California road. The murder of Buffum was the result.

At the erection of John Brown's monument I heard Senator Ingals say, in his speech, "that John Brown and no one else saved Lawrence on that occasion; that John Brown was in command; and but for him it would have been destroyed." The facts are just as you have stated: Gov. Geary and Col. Cooke saved Lawrence.

Public opinion is changing here, notwithstanding Speer and Hanway are going for you. I expect you will go for us all, but let the *facts* come out. It is better for all parties. I could tell you many things confirmatory of your statements in regard to old John Brown, as well as additional thereto.

I remain as ever, Yours,

SAMUEL WALKER.

JOHN BROWN'S FRAUDULENT CABIN.
[SEE PAGE 50.]

REVIEW.

As a fitting conclusion to this APPENDIX, I add a REVIEW, by Hon. ELI THAYER, of Massachusetts. No person watched with greater interest than he every movement in Kansas while freedom and slavery were at issue in that Territory. That the reader may the better comprehend the stand-point from which Mr. T. writes, he will allow me briefly to state, that in 1854 he was a Representative from the city of Worcester, in the Massachusetts Legislature. In January of that year, Mr. T. devised the plan of the Emigrant Company, and in February went with his charter, before the Judiciary Committee, of which Judge Colt, now of the Supreme Court of Massachusetts, was Chairman. Mr. Thayer said in substance before the Committee, that the Kansas-Nebraska bill was sure to become a law; that the country ought to be prepared for it; that the decisive struggle between freedom and slavery was about to transpire; that for many years this contest had been carried on in Congress, with invariable triumph for slavery, and invariable defeat for freedom; that it was time to change the battle ground, and we must be ready to try the issue on the prairies; that if the South gave us fair play, our superior strength and power of organization would give us certain victory; that if slavery would not allow us fair play we were a thousand times more certain to triumph, for while the North was always willing to endure the aggressions of slavery, if made according to law, she would crush all such as were made contrary to law; that the granting of the charter would be the overthrow of slavery, by making Kansas free, and by securing freedom to all our other territories. Thus the political power of slavery would be ended, and, speedily, its life. The Kansas-Nebraska bill became a law on the 30th of May following. Mr. T. had been several months in the field, and had, through the press and forum, thoroughly aroused the New England States. He was made President of the Emigrant Aid Company, and traveled from city to city, addressing the assembled thousands; entrancing them with his powerful eloquence, and arousing the people to a full consciousness of their danger and duty. He induced capitalists to subscribe largely to the stock of the Company, to enable it to encourage the humble pioneer, who, stimulated by a similar zeal for the right, should go forward, and by actual settlement in the Territory, contribute his share towards developing its resources, and in "laying deep and broad the foundations of an empire which shall be sacred to freedom."

With funds thus raised, cheap rates of travel were established; large parties were enabled to travel together for mutual aid and protection; cities were projected and located; the press was encouraged; saw-mills and hotels were built; lumber was furnished at moderate prices; and the destitute were frequently given employment; while worthy agents were kept on the alert, watching with paternal care the development of the infant colonies; and, more than all, were continually active with pamphlets, circulars, newspapers, memorials to Congress, and public addresses, in building up and sustaining a powerful sympathizing and favorable opinion in the States.

Mr. Thayer was the founder, proprietor, and principal of the Oread Institute, in Worcester, a Seminary for the education of young ladies. This he neglected, to his serious pecuniary loss, to give his great labors to the welfare of the future, by excluding slavery and its blighting influences from the plains of Kansas.

When mob violence destroyed Lawrence, the Emigrant Aid Company, with its organized capital and energy, to give cheer to the settlers, set itself at work to speedily re-erect that which was demolished. When arms were needed for defence, careful that the Company, as such, should commit no breach of rights, its members, in their individual capacity, promptly contributed of their means, the necessary money to buy and ship them to Kansas.

In the darkest hour, when others despaired of success, Mr. Thayer was full of hope; wrote cheerful words of encouragement ; and assured all that the result would be fully satisfactory.

Like the great mass of the active friends of Kansas in the Eastern States, Mr. Thayer was deceived by placing confidence in the representations of old John Brown. Ignorant of the full facts until years after, Mr. T. contributed largely of his private means to aid the old man in his insurrectionary movements.

If Mr. Thayer expresses himself forcibly, in hostility to old John Brown, the reader will observe that he was induced, *by falsehood*, to furnish arms to be used in a rebellion against the sovereignty of the United States ; that Hon. Gerritt Smith was driven to insanity, when he learned of the abuse made of his money and confidence furnished in the same direction ; and that Mr. T. felt that he was highly censurable for reposing confidence in his integrity. But I am detaining the reader quite too long with this introduction :

> "One of that saintly, murderous brood,
> "To carnage and the Koran given,
> "Who think through unbelievers' blood
> "Lies their directest path to heaven."

G. W. BROWN, M. D.—DEAR SIR :—Every lover of historical truth owes you a debt of gratitude, for your fearless and manly review of the history of John Brown in Kansas. You have followed the guidance of facts to their logical and indisputable conclusions, unterrified by denunciation and abuse, unmoved by the sickly protests and the sickening entreaties of the sentimental worshippers of the subject of your sketch. That a man so narrow and bigoted as he, so ignorant and deceptive, so ferocious and malignant, should have been puffed into the semblance of a moral hero, or inflated to the majestic stature of a god, is one of the greatest wonders of this wonderful century.

It was fortunate for Kansas that John Brown did not enter her borders till the time had passed when he, or any other man, could have changed her destiny. Had he come one year earlier, his blind ferocity, and unreasoning hatred of slave holders, might have subjected our infant colonies to retaliatory acts by Missourians, which they would have been powerless either to resist or avert.

Still more fortunate would it have been for that afflicted Territory if he had never come at all. He had nothing in common with the Free State settlers, and came, not as they, to make a free State, but to incite a Northern rebellion against the government of the Union. He confessed his failure to accomplish that purpose, and left the Territory after he had been entreated to do so by Gov. Crawford, and other prominent Free State men. The busy pens of a few Northern disunionists recorded his departure as a great loss to the Free State Council ! When was John Brown ever seen in Council ? When was his advice on public measures ever solicited? Did President Lincoln ask the counsel of Tom Hyer, the pugilist, concerning the war of the Union?

According to Mr. Redpath, John Brown despised Councils, but was always ready to fight. In Dickens' "Domby & Son" appears a like character,—Chicken, the boxer,—whose only inquiry was always: "Is there any body to be doubled up?" In studying the method of "doubling up" somebody John Brown found "scope and verge enough" for all his intellectual ability. He could not have understood, if he would, the philosophy of that organization which made Kansas a free State, and which, from its first action, gave assurance of its ultimate success, in strict accordance with the law and the Constitution.

As the case now stands, but little more may be said of John Brown. No one need paint again the ghastly picture on the Pottawotomie! Five unarmed men, taken from their homes at midnight, and murdered in cold blood! The supplicating agony of wives and children, soon changing to the despairing wail of widows and orphans! Five dead bodies lying unattended on the bleak prairie, with heads split open, hands cut off, breast and jaws punctured, and the curdling blood crying from the ground for vengeance! An appalling scene! One more hideous than this could scarcely be presented to mortal eye. Friends and eulogists can never palliate, or explain away, the damning infamy and fiendish atrocity of the doers of this horrid work. As that picture is now presented, so it must remain forever! Invincible truth will be its keeper, and no friend of the great criminal can throw light on its deep shadows, or erase a single one of its loathsome features. Neither can it be made worse. The concentrated malice of all Brown's enemies, with unlimited license to do their will, could add nothing to its overwhelming horrors! No one need again expose to public execration that merciless tyranny which drove one of his sons through murder to insanity, and two others through treason to death!

In that brief portion of Brown's history which is before the public, there are some cases of "conspicuous inexactness," which contrast very strikingly with that "eminent truthfulness," so fervidly described and so tenaciously dwelt upon by his admiring eulogists:

1. He told F. B. Sanborn and many others that he was not present at the Pottawotomie massacre. It is proved that he was present as commander of the midnight assassins.

2. He repeatedly affirmed that he took no part in the killing, though he approved of it. It is proved that he slew with his own hands one of the hapless and helpless victims!

3. He asserted that in his Missouri raid he liberated several slaves without bloodshed and without the use of weapons. It is in proof that one respectable and quiet farmer was murdered in that raid, by one of Brown's men.

4. Before his attack upon the United States' arsenal, at Harper's Ferry, he spent several weeks in Virginia. He pretended to be a mineralogist, and went about with a hammer breaking off the corners of rocks. Under the pretext of seeking for copper he found opportunities for trying to enlist slaves in his little rebellion. These facts were narrated to me by a representative in Congress from the Harper's Ferry district.

5. The surveyor trick is already well understood. It was of the same character with his mineralogical observations.

6. While he was in Massachusetts, in 1857-'58, I repeatedly heard him recite his "Capture of Henry Clay Pate." He gave the same rendition of that highly interesting story several times a day while he was here, describing the same incidents with minute exactness in the same identical language. The substance of his narrative was, that he met Clay Pate on the open prairie; that he had nine men on foot, and Pate twenty-seven on horse-back, and that he captured Pate and his entire command. When asked why Pate did not wheel about and ride away, Brown said: "We received three rounds without harm from Pate's men while marching towards them. We then fired and two or three of Pate's men fell from their horses. Then they all seemed stupefied. Leaving my men I went oer to Pate and held my pistol to his head commanding him to surrender. He surrend-

ered!" Then followed the clinching pantomime of drawing from one of his boots a huge bowie knife with the name of Pate engraved upon the handle. No allusion was ever made in these recitals, in my hearing, to Capt. Shore, or Capt. Mewhinny, or to their men. It may be his "kindness of heart" restrained any utterance which might have exposed the two Captains, and their companies, to retaliatory measures from Missouri.

7. The writer's confidence has been many times abused, but never in any other instance so grossly and wickedly abused as by John Brown. Not long before his attack on the United States arsenal he came to my house to ask for arms, with which, he said, he intended to protect some Free State settlements in Kansas, against an invasion of Border Ruffians, at that very time in process of preparation. He would not tell me how he had ascertained the fact of the intended raid, or what was the proof of it. He said he knew it and would like to be prepared to save our settlements. I gave him all the arms I had. I did not hear of him, or the arms in Kansas, or of any invasion of Border Ruffians, but I did hear of his attack *upon the United States' Arsenal, at Harper's Ferry, with these identical arms,* which were there captured. In this way he made my devotion to the free State settlements in Kansas, serve to aid and abet his own *Treason* in Virginia. Had he told me the TRUTH, effective measures would have been taken to prevent his suicidal and murderous work. When the end justifies the means *lying may be a holy vocation!*

So in all these transactions John Brown may have thought he was doing God's service. Ignorant, infatuated, intolerant,—the ripest growth of Garrisonian disunionism,—he had the daring to do what the others of his school had only courage to resolve, to wit: that,

"The time has fully come for the people to practically assert their right of revolution."

John Brown threw away his life in a futile effort to translate into heroic deeds the graceless gabble of a few Northern Secessionists. Stimulated by their sentiments, and exasperated almost to frenzy by his attempts and failures in Kansas to sustain them, he determined to rush, single-handed, against the power of the United States. Cervantes himself never wrote any thing one-half so Quixotic. If John Brown did not know that this was suicide he knew less than any other sane man in the country. But it was suicide, such as might be supposed to have attractions for a man of his obstinate ambition and adverse experience. It was suicide, to be justified by the teachings of disunion societies; to be sanctified by its simulation of martyrdom; to be glorified by all the abolition secessionists in the free States.

Some charitable people say that our "hero" was insane, but there seems to have been "too much method for madness." His disease appears to have been rather moral than mental, and of that kind that could not have been economically cured in any swine-producing country near the sea. But whether sane, or insane, he acted well the part of *heavy villain* in the Kansas drama. Now "his soul goes marching on!" Well, let it march—until it shall become infinitely remote!

WORCESTER, Mass., Jan. 13th, 1880.   ELI THAYER.

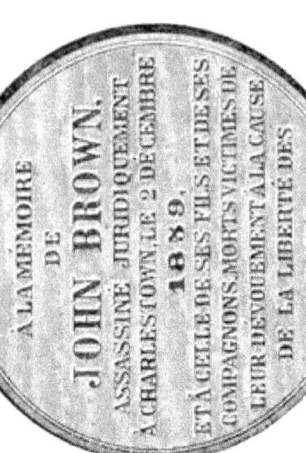

FRENCH MEDAL TO THE BROWN FAMILY.

INDEX.

Dedication,	v	An interlude,	39
Introduction,	vi	A strange coincidence,	40
Correspondence,	vi	Further strategy,	41
Prefatory,	3	An exciting incident,	41
Explanatory,	4	The terrible fate of a typo,	43
First notice of John Brown in Kan. His.,	5	Brewerton,	44
Acquaintance with the Sons,	6	A first class bore,	46
The Wakarusa war,	6	The letter-writers,	48
John Brown in Lawrence,	7	John Brown's cabin a fraud,	50
Capt. Charley Lenhart,	9	The home of John Brown,	50
Personal to the writer,	9	A glance in passing,	51
History of a revolver,	11	Return to Kansas,	52
Sacking of Lawrence—Arrests,	12	An important letter,	53
Horrible murders on the Pottawotomie,	12	Kansas too hot for him,	54
Details of the massacre,	13	Osawotomie Brown,	56
Incidents of history,	14	Not all bad,	57
Who was responsible for the massacre,	16	Confirmation,	58
Further, who was responsible,	17	The clincher,	59
Newly discovered evidence,	19	Chance for correction,	60
Terrible arraignment,	20	Corrections,	61
Motive for the killing,	21	The fly on the locomotive,	64
Too good to murder,	22	Hero worship,	65
Effect of massacre on Free State praty,	22	Conclusion,	65
Effect not limited to Kansas,	26	Appendix,	67
The Summer of 1856,	27	Letter of Mr. Thayer,	67
John Brown's biographer,	28	Letter of Gov. Crawford,	67
John Brown, Jr.,	30	Potawoto'e massacre, Col. Blood's letter,	68
Gov. Geary,	32	Statement of the Grants,	71
A crisis approaching,	32	Were they mutilated,	72
Another invasion,	33	Mr. Townsley's statement,	72
Federal interposition,	34	Confirmatory letter of Col. Walker,	75
The pro-slavery account,	36	Review,	77
Redpath's statement,	36	Introductory notice of Mr. Thayer,	77
Capt. Brown's statement,	38	Eli Thayer's Review,	78

ILLUSTRATIONS:

Capt. John Brown,	Face Title Page.
John Brown's Fraudulent Cabin,	76
French Medal to the Brown Family,	81

OF

OLD JOHN BROWN.

THRILLING INCIDENTS

OF

BORDER LIFE IN KANSAS;

WITH AN APPENDIX,

CONTAINING STATEMENTS, AND FULL DETAILS OF THE POTTAWOTOMIE MASSACRE, BY GOV. CRAWFORD, COL. BLOOD, JAS. TOWNSLEY, COL. WALKER, AND OTHERS, TO WHICH IS ADDED

A REVIEW: BY HON. ELI THAYER, OF MASSACHUSETTS.

BY G. W. BROWN, M. D.

Where thou findest a lie that is oppressing thee extinguish it. Lies exist only to be extinguished. They wait and cry earnestly for extinction. Think well, meanwhile, in what spirit thou wilt do it: not with hatred; not with headlong, selfish violence; but in clearness of heart, with holy zeal, gently, almost with pity.—CARLYLE.

Let Truth and Falsehood grapple. Who ever knew Truth put to the worse in a free and open encounter?—MILTON.

ROCKFORD, ILLINOIS:
STEREOTYPED AND PRINTED BY ABRAHAM E. SMITH.
1880.